RELIGIOUS DISSEN'

Religious Dissent in East Anglia

Historical Perspectives

The Proceedings of the Second Symposium on the History of Religious Dissent in East Anglia

Edited by
Norma Virgoe and Tom Williamson

Norfolk Archaeological and
Historical Research Group

and

Centre of East Anglian Studies
University of East Anglia
1993

© Individual Authors 1993

ISBN 0 906219 31 0

All rights reserved. No part of this publication may be reproduced, stored in a retrieval system, or transmitted, in any form or by any means, electronic, mechanical, photocopying, recording, or otherwise, without permission of the publisher.

Published by The Centre of East Anglian Studies, University of East Anglia, Norwich

Printed by The Printing Unit, University of East Anglia, Norwich

Contents

List of Contributors
p.7
Introduction
p.9

Christopher Stell
Nonconformist Chapels in East Anglia
p.11

Raingard Esser
The Politijcke Mannen: A Particular Institution of the Norwich Strangers' Communities
p.21

William Woods
Publications Connected with the Dutch Church in Norwich
p.29

William Jacob
Evidence for Dissent in Norfolk 1711-1800 from the Records of the Diocese of Norwich
p.37

Janet Ede and Norma Virgoe
Mapping Nonconformity in Norfolk
p.47

Tom Williamson
The Norfolk Nonconformist Chapels Survey: Some Preliminary Results
p.59

Alun Howkins
Politics or Quietism: the Social History of Nonconformity
p.73

Clyde Binfield
An Excursion into Architectural Cousinhood: the East Anglian Connexion
p.93

Shorter Contributions

John Craig
The Brownists in Bury St Edmunds
p.142

Gwen Dyke
The Relationship of Early Market Towns and Nonconformist Centres to Nineteenth-Century Industrial Development in Suffolk
p.144

Michael Farrar
Records of Nonconformity in Cambridgeshire
p.150

Albert Allcock
The Documentary Problems in Researching the History of Aylsham Baptist Church
p.154

John Le Grice
A Nonconformist Descent
p.156

Violet Rowe
A Quaker in Local Politics: William Graveson 1862-1939
p.159

Index
p.161

List of Contributors

Albert Allcock	Retired Baptist Minister
Clyde Binfield	Department of History, University of Sheffield
John Craig	Peterhouse College, University of Cambridge
Gwen Dyke	Suffolk historian and teacher of local history
Janet Ede	Norfolk Chapels Survey, Norfolk Archaeological and Historical Research Group
Raingard Esser	Institute of Anglo-American History, University of Cologne
Michael Farrar	County Archivist, Cambridgeshire County Record Office
Alun Howkins	School of Cultural and Community Studies, University of Sussex
William Jacob	Lincoln Theological College, Lincoln
John Le Grice	Family Historian
Violet Rowe	Hertfordshire local historian
Christopher Stell	Consultant, Royal Commission on Historical Monuments, England
Norma Virgoe	Norfolk Chapels Survey, Norfolk Archaeological and Historical Research Group
Tom Williamson	Centre of East Anglian Studies, University of East Anglia
William Woods	Director of the Dutch and Flemish Studies Centre, Norwich

List of Contributors

Albert Allcock	Retired Baptist Minister
Clyde Binfield	Department of History, University of Sheffield
John Craig	Peterhouse College, University of Cambridge
Gwen Dyke	Suffolk historian and teacher of local history
Janet Ede	Norfolk Chapels Survey, Norfolk Archaeological and Historical Research Group
Raingard Esser	Institute of Anglo-American History, University of Cologne
Michael Farrar	County Archivist, Cambridgeshire County Record Office
Alun Howkins	School of Cultural and Community Studies, University of Sussex
William Jacob	Lincoln Theological College, Lincoln
John Le Grice	Family Historian
Violet Rowe	Hertfordshire local historian
Christopher Stell	Consultant, Royal Commission on Historical Monuments, England
Norma Virgoe	Norfolk Chapels Survey, Norfolk Archaeological and Historical Research Group
Tom Williamson	Centre of East Anglian Studies, University of East Anglia
William Woods	Director of the Dutch and Flemish Studies Centre, Norwich

INTRODUCTION

The *Second Symposium on the History of Religious Dissent in East Anglia* was held at the Centre of East Anglian Studies at the University of East Anglia, Norwich, from the 12 to the 14 April 1991. It was organised by the Norfolk Archaeological and Historical Research Group.

Norwich was a most appropriate place for such a meeting for the city has a long history of active Dissent. Lollardy was strong here in the later Middle Ages and the city was staunchly Parliamentarian in its loyalties throughout the Civil War. In the eighteenth and early nineteenth centuries, it was the focus for the great flowering of Norfolk Methodism. Yet not only was nonconformity strong in the city: Dissenters also dissented bitterly and frequently from each other. In 1759 John Wesley, writing in his journal of one of his Norwich congregations, reported that he had 'Told them in plain terms that they were the most ignorant, self-conceited, self-willed, fickle, untractable, disorderly, disjointed society' that he had ever encountered and that he was determined to 'end them or mend them'.

Unlike so many of the early congregations, our conference did not reach a point of irreconcilable schism, although several of the lectures provoked lively and lengthy debate and argument. The majority of the papers presented at the meeting are reproduced in this volume. Some are by professional historians, others by noted amateur students of the subject: all demonstrate the vitality of nonconformist studies in the region. The ground they cover is wide and diverse. Sixteenth-century nonconformity in Norwich and Bury St Edmunds is discussed in the contributions by John Craig, Raingard Esser and William Woods, while the development and geographical distribution of dissenting congregations in later centuries is examined in papers by Janet Ede and Norma Virgoe, by Gwen Dyke and by William Jacob. The nineteenth century 'culture of chapel' is discussed by Alun Howkins, while Violet Rose and John Le Grice present brief biographical and genealogical case studies, and Michael Farrar and Bert Allcock discuss the sources available for the study of nonconformity. This second symposium saw a greater emphasis than the first on the architecture of nonconformity. Christopher Stell offers a broad overview of the development of chapel

INTRODUCTION

architecture in the region, while Tom Williamson presents an examination of the Norfolk evidence and Clyde Binfield contributes a detailed and scholarly twentieth-century case study.

Conventions such as this, however, offer something more than a chance to hear varied collections of informative lectures. They also provide an opportunity for lively informal contact, for the exchange of views and information. The success of the conference owed much to the contributions, in discussion and argument, of those who are not represented here - the general participants. The history of nonconformity in East Anglia is a field of lively interest and we look forward with keen anticipation to the third conference in this series which is to be held in Suffolk.

We would like to thank Mavis Wesley for typing the text of this volume, Phillip Judge for drawing the maps, Janet Ede for sharing with us the work of organising the conference and above all George Fenner for masterminding the whole event with his customary combination of skill, fortitude and good humour.

October 1992

NORMA VIRGOE
TOM WILLIAMSON

NONCONFORMIST CHAPELS IN EAST ANGLIA

CHRISTOPHER STELL

Glemsford in Suffolk may not seem the most obvious of places from which to commence even the most superficial of ramblings amongst a few of the more notable East Anglian chapels and meeting-houses; but every picture and every village tells a tale. In 1971 two Baptist chapels stood in Glemsford just a short distance apart. The older of the two, 'Ebenezer', dated 1829, was then still in use, its rendered walls, sash windows and hipped roof giving it a distinctly homely appearance. The other, named 'Providence' and dated 1859 on strips of board fixed above the entrance, had fallen on evil times. Its cheaply Gothic lancet windows in red and yellow brick still attempted to convey the popular though ill-conceived perception of a place of worship long after the spirit had departed. Through the broken glass could still be seen the chapel furniture, but it was mouldering fast and thick with the excrement of birds. Lush growths of elder rose from the floor, a line of hat pegs could be seen on a distant wall above the peeling brown paint of a matchboarded dado; and so could a broad brown rostrum pulpit, silent now, its strangely Quakerly appearance enhanced by facing pews. All have now gone. By 1977, Providence had given place to a private house, though remarkably, and thankfully, its little burial-ground remained in good condition. Ebenezer lasted longer, but in 1986 it too was threatened with demolition and a whole facet of the religious life of the village was faced with extinction and oblivion.

The fate of the Glemsford chapels is one which has befallen many others in recent times and is a stern reminder of the transient nature of buildings when interest in them wanes and neglect or apathy gains the upper hand. Protestant Dissent in England is older than any surviving chapels although many extant examples still recall for us earlier buildings or events connected with their history. At Laxfield in Suffolk the early nineteenth-century Strict Baptist chapel carries on its front wall a tablet commemorating John Noyes who suffered martyrdom in 1557 for his support of the Protestant cause. It is one of several such memorials in the country most of which were erected within the last century and a half. The later sixteenth century saw the gradual growth of religious factions, at first within and then outside the established church, a movement which the Conventicle Act of 1593 attempted ineffectually to stifle. Some groups moved for a time to Amsterdam, Leyden or other continental cities whence, in 1612, came some returning refugees to set up the first Baptist congregation in England. Although the Quakers were relative late-comers on the scene, emerging during the disturbed and disorientated period of the Commonwealth, one of the oldest buildings occupied by a nonconformist society in East Anglia is their meeting-house in Great Yarmouth. Plain, rather dull and much rebuilt though it now is, it still incorporates a fragment of a house of the Austin Friars, and is a good illustration of the kind of converted building which was often the first home of an emerging congregation.

Another, better known and far more spectacularly converted building, is the Independent or Congregational meeting-house at Walpole in Suffolk. This seems to have originated as a private house perhaps in the sixteenth century, a timber-framed and plastered building with a broad frontage and gabled ends. In the late seventeenth century it was fitted out as a meeting-house and enlarged to the rear giving the building double gables to the end walls while still retaining its very domestic appearance. Of all English meeting-houses Walpole is amongst the first rank not only externally, but for the remarkable interior in which so many fittings survive - fittings which in any wealthy congregation would have long since vanished; and the meeting-house too, would probably have disappeared in exchange for something over which the Victorian Society might enthuse, but which might equally have proved a sorry substitute for that which had gone. Traces of the structural enlargement at Walpole remain visible in the framing of the end walls; the line of the valley rafter of the re-made roof is marked internally by a row of three tall supporting columns, while the pulpit with its ponderous sounding-board stands sentinel between a pair of typically large round-arched chapel windows in the back wall. Even the box pews on the lower floor remain largely intact, although the big square pews against the front wall had a very close shave early in the twentieth century when the village carpenter was instructed to remove them - a task which, with solid good sense, he refused to carry out. Even the lighting is worth a second glance: a simple chandelier with its stripy wooden ball and thin metal sconces contrasts with paraffin lamps of a later period, for even they have not yet succeeded in ousting the candles.

The development of nonconformist congregations in our larger towns and cities followed the common pattern of temporary premises succeeded by one or more permanent buildings, rebuilt or enlarged as the changing needs of the congregation required. The Presbyterian congregation in Norwich presents a classic example of the way in which the accommodation of a society changed over a period of a century or so. This congregation had been gathered by John Collinges who was ejected from the living of St Stephen's in 1662. In 1672, at the time of Charles II's Indulgence, the Presbyterians were able to take a lease from the Corporation of the East Granary behind St Andrew's Hall. This building seems to have remained in their occupation until about 1688 when, with Toleration at least in sight, they built a new meeting-house. This was a large building, said to have accommodated a thousand worshippers. A sketch made of it in 1723 by Thomas Kirkpatrick for his *Prospect of Norwich* shows that it had brick walls, a pantiled roof with central valley and a double-gabled rear wing. It lasted a mere sixty-eight years, until 1756, when it was succeeded by the Octagon Chapel which now occupies its site.

Barely one hundred yards away from the Norwich Octagon lies the Old Meeting-house. The Independent congregation there traces its history back to 1644 when a joint church with adherents in Norwich and Great Yarmouth separated into its two basic elements. During the Commonwealth the Norwich congregation had the use of the parish church of St George, Tombland, and after the upheaval of the Restoration they found a home for a time in the West Granary of the Blackfriars Monastery, before moving soon after 1685 to a brewing house in St Edmund's parish. Their first permanent meeting-house, which fortunately still survives and which is one of the most important of its kind in the country, was begun sometime after 1688 and completed by 1693. Although on a site almost hidden from the road it is finished in an elaborate manner with delicately carved Corinthian capitals to the pilasters of the front wall and richly detailed canopies to the two doorways, features which can hardly be called Puritan or plain.

A third great Norwich meeting-house, though unfortunately a casualty of war-time bombing, was the Friends' meeting-house at the Guildencroft. This was slightly later in date than the Old Meeting, being built in 1698, but its brick front with pilasters and two tiers of windows, although less elaborate, still bore a striking resemblance to the earlier building. A fragment of the Guildencroft still exists, about five bays at half their original height, now incorporated in a rebuilt meeting-house.

Ipswich has also had its share of nonconformist buildings of many dates and denominations though not all have survived to tell their tale. By far the most important is the St Nicholas Street or Friars' Street meeting-house, built in 1700 for a Presbyterian congregation which, as with many others in England, gradually became Unitarian. The original approach to this building is from St Nicholas Street through a narrow passageway between shops which must have stood there even before the meeting-house was built. The building has timber-framed walls rendered in plaster with carved details to the door cases comparable in quality to those of the Old Meeting in Norwich. The front of the building, as it is usually seen today, faces Friars' Street where the old burial-ground has succumbed to the evil modern practice of levelling and letting out for car parking! A useful article on this and the slightly later chapel in Bury St Edmunds appeared in the *Archaeological Journal* for 1951 together with a transcription of the building contract between the members of the building committee or trustees and the builder Joseph Clarke of Ipswich who is described as a 'house carpenter'. The ground dimensions of the building are given as fifty feet by sixty feet and the internal height as twenty-one feet from floor to ceiling. The total estimated cost was £257, together with 'four barrels of good small Beere for to drink whilst Imployed in the said buildings' for Joseph Clarke and his men. The contract states that the double roof is 'to be boorne up in the middle with four good substanciall Cullums' which still do good service. Two of these are freestanding, the others are on the same alignment but incorporated in the gallery fronts. The St Nicholas Street meeting-house was visited in 1720 by Daniel Defoe who says 'it is as large and as fine a building of that kind as most on this side of England, and the inside the best finished of any I have seen, London not excepted'. Of particular note is the finely carved pulpit with a staircase leading up to it and a very magnificent chandelier, once a standard piece of chapel equipment of which all too few examples now remain.

One more seventeenth-century East Anglian meeting-house which must not go unnoticed, although now greatly altered, is that at Guestwick in Norfolk. It stands forlorn, disused and derelict in the middle of a field though destined now it seems for conversion to a house with all the risks that this entails, not least to the survival of the innocent little burial-ground where, for three centuries, the Dissenting families of the village have been

laid to rest. Nothing is known of the first meeting-place of the Independent church of Guestwick except that it was 'altered and rebuilt' in 1695 on the insistence of a new minister, and it is presumably this structure which is incorporated in the present building. Sufficient remains to show that it was timber-framed with two posts supporting the roof. Its exterior was later cased in brickwork partly in the eighteenth century but principally, including the main front, in 1840, in an accomplished neo-Tudor style. The inside was also thoroughly refitted at the same time though some of the structural woodwork may be earlier. The main columns supporting the roof could themselves be nineteenth-century replacements, but evidence for curved braces running from the ends of the main longitudinal beam down to posts which are still concealed in the walls sufficiently attests to the survival of earlier work. Box pews continued to be built here in the 1840 refitting and the lasting impression is of a conscious intention by the restorers to retain at least the semblance of an early meeting-house.

Such was hardly the case at Wattisfield, Suffolk where another Independent congregation, almost equally as old as Guestwick, built a large timber-framed meeting-house in 1706. This was pulled down in 1876 and a new chapel built on the site which although described as 'a pattern of what a village chapel should be' is a sad replacement for what might have been a second Walpole.

Some of the best brickwork in nonconformist architecture is to be found at Bury St Edmunds, in Churchgate Street Chapel, built in 1711 for a Presbyterian congregation. The site had been acquired soon after the Act of Toleration with the intention of replacing an existing house, but the new work was delayed for twenty years, perhaps because of the cost, and meanwhile the house then on the site served for meetings. It is interesting to note that the cost of building Churchgate Street Chapel was just over £832 compared with £257 for St Nicholas Street, Ipswich, a larger though timber building, only a dozen years before. The Bury Chapel has lost a small pediment above the front elevation which ought to be put back in order to complete an otherwise perfect and unspoilt frontage. The interior is almost square in plan with a central post supporting the roof aided by further columns which rise up through the front of the surrounding galleries. Early in this century, perhaps when the pediment was lopped off, the lower seating was also cleared away and screens erected below the gallery fronts. Fortunately, however, the numbered gallery seats have remained largely intact as well as the tall pulpit which faces the entrance. A much plainer meeting-house at Framlingham, also of brick and built for Presbyterians in 1717, only six years after that at Bury St Edmunds, illustrates the considerable differences that can be found between the building erected by the wealthiest congregations and those built by those of more limited means. Framlingham expresses that domestic simplicity with which most congregations had to be content. As with almost all chapels of that period it has the entrances on the longer front wall with the pulpit opposite. Also, typically and regrettably, we find that it was 'reordered' in the nineteenth century when the interior was changed about, the pulpit moved to one end, a gallery removed and one of the entrances rendered useless.

The early eighteenth century also saw the erection of a new meeting-house in Ipswich. The Independents who had previously formed a joint congregation with the Presbyterians separated from them in 1686 and began meeting in a rented building in the Green Yard, where they soon afterwards built a meeting-house. In 1718 they bought land for a larger building in Tacket Street and this was opened in September 1720. It was a building of moderate size, forty-five feet by forty feet, built of brick, which Daniel Defoe visited soon after it was finished. He was not over-enthusiastic, comparing it unfavourably with the Presbyterian meeting-house in St Nicholas Street; 'it is a handsome new built building, but not so gay or so large as the other'. It was fitted out as usual with the pulpit between tall windows at the back and with the then customary pair of timber columns to support the roof. These were presented to the meeting by a Mr Barnard, an Ipswich merchant, and were claimed plausibly enough to have come from a man-of-war. This building lasted until 1857 when a newly appointed minister made it a condition of his coming that a new chapel should be built.

The early eighteenth-century Independent chapel at Oulton in Norfolk has been more fortunate and the neglect it suffered for many years may have been its means of salvation. It stands on a remote site not far from Irmingland Hall, the seat of Lieutenant General Fleetwood, son-in-law of Oliver Cromwell. There the private chapel was long used as a place of worship for Dissenters for whom a nonconformist chaplain was employed. The congregation which worshipped at the hall was originally united with Guestwick, but separated in 1724 and in the first flush of independence built themselves a new chapel about one mile to the east which was opened in 1731. Brick now seems to have become the accepted building material and the double-gabled side walls were given shaped Dutch gables for additional effect. The front has suffered a degree of modernisation for sash window frames have replaced the older cross-framed casements, but the older sort remain at the sides. The interior again has the two column support to the roof, columns which are sometimes referred to as 'Jachin and Boaz' after the pillars of Solomon's Temple. Around three sides runs the gallery, still with its original seating, but lower down some untoward changes have been made: the once grand pulpit has been superseded by a kind of square 'witness box' while the finely inlaid hexagonal panel from the underside of the sounding-board has been roughly nailed to the back wall. Nevertheless, these tinkerings apart, a century of poverty has probably caused less damage than a century of affluence.

The mid eighteenth century is represented by the former Congregational chapel at Rendham, Suffolk, built in 1750, though its closure about 1972 and subsequent sale, internal stripping and various unsympathetic proposals for domestic conversion have destroyed yet another irreplaceable part of our nonconformist heritage. Enlargement in 1834 to accommodate a growing congregation meant that the front, though possibly still following the former design, was brought forward by twelve feet. The original building, thirty-eight feet in width, was only about thirty feet deep, so continuing the long-established tradition of broad-fronted chapels. Before the trustees succeeded in ridding themselves of yet another unloved encumbrance the original pulpit still remained in place with its pedimented back-board, a feature which was then, in the middle decades of the eighteenth-century, gradually replacing the large canopied sounding-boards of the earlier meeting-houses. So, too, did the music stands fixed to each end of the communion table. These added a bucolic touch, recalling the days when the grandfather of the last church treasurer was precentor, officiating from behind the table in the days before chapel organs arrived to drown all lesser means of musical accompaniment.

Quaker meeting-houses stand a little apart from other buildings of Protestant Dissent, both in their design and in their mode of use. Two call for particular mention here; one, to all intents and purposes, destroyed, the other standing and in use. The older of the two, built in the late seventeenth century, is in Woodbridge. It is a listed building, but so rendered up and 'modernised' on the outside in the nineteenth century that all its external character has been lost. Inside, however, even after many years of use as a builder's store, the exceptionally rich furnishings had, until recently, survived remarkably intact. Opposite the entrance was the long raised bench for the accredited ministers and elders, with panelled front and two short staircases, their handrails supported by intricately turned and twisted balusters; at each end of the room was a high gallery held up by delicate columns and flights of stairs, again with twisted balusters bearing witness to the refined taste which dared even here to adorn simplicity with curlicues. What now is left after conversion to yet another house? A few brick walls! All else is swept away - the bath water is kept, the baby's down the drain!

A happier tale may be told of the second meeting-house, at Swafield in Norfolk. This is a square brick building of 1772, much later than Woodbridge. This, however, has remained in use and has not suffered greatly over the years from the attention of those improvers who delight to alter what they do not understand. Beneath the steep pyramidal roof lies the single room which is the principal accommodation, lit at the front by two tiers of windows. Inside, the platform for the elders faces the entrance. To right and left of the outer door are twin staircases to the single gallery, running across the front of the building. The most remarkable feature here is the seating in the gallery, plain backless benches clearly intended for the children of the meeting. Bisecting them, axially above the entrance, a tall partition separated boys from girls. As so often happens a gradual decline has left untouched the galleries and their fittings when all else may have been swept away. Swafield has been fortunate in receiving a repair grant from English Heritage, something which hopefully indicates an awareness of the importance of such a building, an importance which extends beyond the basic needs of those who still gather for worship within it.

What may well be described as the greatest event to take place in the development of nonconformist architecture, certainly in the second half of the eighteenth century, took place in Norwich with the rebuilding in 1756 of the Presbyterian chapel. The new Octagon Chapel was a great departure for nonconformists who had hitherto been content with rectangular buildings fitted out as the local 'house carpenter' or builder was best able to do. Here, at last, we have a carefully designed building by a known architect, Thomas Ivory, which, although perhaps not entirely original, was sufficiently unusual to excite general comment. One of those who visited it soon after its erection was John Wesley who described it in his *Journal* for 23 December 1757:

> I was shewn Dr Taylor's new meeting-house, perhaps the most elegant one in all Europe. It is eight square, built of the finest brick, with sixteen sash-windows below, as many above, and eight sky-lights in the dome, which

indeed are purely ornamental. The inside is finished in the highest taste, and is as clean as any nobleman's saloon. The communion-table is fine mahogany; the latches of the pew doors are polished brass.

The interior is certainly impressive with its ring of eight tall Corinthian columns; although these have been repainted; traces of an earlier light marbled finish remain visible below the later pulpit platform. It was a very expensive chapel to build, costing over £5,000 - about twenty times the sum spent on St Nicholas Street, Ipswich, some fifty-six years earlier, a considerable increase even allowing for inflation. Some of the extra cost must have gone into the complicated carpentry of the roof and this may be one of the reasons why this design was not more widely copied. In fact John Wesley recommended its use for his own Methodist chapels, but these were less ambitious in their decoration and, even so, some of the local builders found the intricacies of the roof carpentry beyond their abilities. Independents and Baptists also tried their hands at building octagons, sometimes regular but often in elongated form; one of these was a Baptist chapel at Stoke Green, Ipswich, unfortunately pulled down a few decades ago. The most unusual variant of the polygonal plan appeared in the following century in Suffolk. At Fressingfield in 1835, and a few years later at Friston, two very similar Strict Baptist chapels were built as elongated hexagons, sometimes referred to as 'coffin-shaped'.

There can be no doubt that, however interesting these variations in plan form may have been and however well they served to display the versatility of their designers, they were poorly adapted for their intended use. Enlargement, often called for by growing congregations, was relatively simple in a rectangular building, but with an octagon or hexagon very much more building work was required. It may be argued that the square plan is as closely related to other regular polygons as it is to the ubiquitous rectangle. It was as versatile and no more complex in construction than the latter and it is surprising that it does not occur more frequently, though it is by no means rare. One of the best examples is the late eighteenth-century Methodist chapel in Little Walsingham which stands almost concealed from view behind other buildings at one end of the main street. It is a brick building of 1794 with a pyramidal roof covered with dark glazed pantiles and, at the apex, a curly-tailed weathervane, one of only a surprisingly small number to be found on nonconformist chapels. The front wall has a doorway with a pedimented doorcase which would not be out of place on any good Georgian house, but the two tiers of round-arched windows seem to have just a little more of 'chapel' about them. Inside, the very deep gallery around three sides has, predictably, all its early box pews still intact, but nineteenth-century improvers have replaced the pulpit, strengthened the gallery supports by substituting cast-iron, and reseated the lower floor - unless, that is, they simply added pews in a space which may at first just have been occupied by plain loose benches.

Interest in East Anglian chapels is by no means exhausted by the end of the eighteenth century. The nineteenth century also produced its great buildings, great in size if not always in quality. One such was the 'Primitive Methodist Temple' in Great Yarmouth built in 1875 and overlooking Priory Plain. Pairs of tall Corinthian columns carrying lengths of moulded entablature seemed to bear little relationship to the big plain pediment which topped the elevation; perhaps its builders suffered from *folie de grandeur*, but it played no insignificant part in the townscape and its loss must surely still be felt. More generally acceptable were the Gothic revival buildings such as the new Tacket Street chapel in Ipswich of 1857 or the Presbyterian chapel in Portman Road in the same town, both designed by Frederick Barnes. Few names of nationally acclaimed architects appear amongst the designers of these later chapels, but one important exception cannot be overlooked; Edwin Lutyens' little Methodist chapel at Overstrand on the Norfolk coast, built in 1898, is a masterpiece which proves that size is not everything. There are other small nineteenth-century chapels in East Anglia also worth searching out, though few can surpass in rustic charm the rudely pinnacled builder's gothic of the 1844 Whepstead Baptist chapel near Bury St Edmunds.

Many moving stories are attached to these village chapels, some written down, others fast fading from folk memory - literally moving in the case of the Primitive Methodist chapel at Melton, Suffolk, for this is one of the earliest examples of a building bodily transported on rollers to a new site, an event which took place in 1860 and which is attested by contemporary photographs. More poignant is the record of the funeral in 1813 of Thomas Smith, the first minister at Shelfanger, Norfolk, whose table tomb stands in the chapel forecourt. Down the street in procession came the chapel singers chanting a funeral dirge, after them comes Pastor Smith's own waggon carrying the coffin, drawn by his own team of horses, a waggon tilt on the coffin for a pall, his children in deep mourning seated around and, at the rear, attached to the waggon by the bridle, the chief mourner, Pastor Smith's riding horse.

Truly 'that which decayeth and waxeth old is ready to vanish away' (Hebrews 8.13).

THE *POLITIJCKE MANNEN*: A PARTICULAR INSTITUTION OF THE NORWICH STRANGERS' COMMUNITIES

RAINGARD ESSER

On the 1st November 1565 the city authorities received Letters Patent from Queen Elizabeth I granting 'Therty Douchemen'[1] the right to live and work in Norwich. The charter regulated the size and character of the immigrant community and defined its economic activities. The precise details of how its social and economic activities were to be controlled were, however, left to the city authorities.

For the Norwich city fathers the Strangers' churches were the essential means of communication between the English and the refugees. Both the Dutch and Walloon churches in Norwich were founded according to the example of the London Dutch church. The religious base of their discipline was Johannes à Lasco's *Forma ac ratio* with its set of ecclesiastical rules and regulations and its institutions of ministers, elders and deacons who were responsible for social and religious order in the community.[2] Ministers and elders of the Dutch and Walloon churches were regarded by the authorities as guarantors of a self-sufficient, independent social organisation who could be addressed in cases of disputes.

However, both the regulations laid down in the charter and the required submission under church discipline, were not sufficient to deal with the problems posed by the enormous influx of refugees into Norwich in the late 1560s. In 1568 a visitation made by order of the Bishop of Norwich counted

---

[1] Norfolk Record Office (NRO). The Norwich Dutch and Walloon Strangers' Book (DWSB). 17d, fol.16

[2] Johannes à Lasco, *Forma ac ratio*, first published 1555 in Frankfort, ed. A. Kuyper, vol.2, Amsterdam, 1866

no less than 1132 Flemish and 339 Walloon refugees in the city.[3] The same year, Mayor Thomas Whalle set down further trade restrictions and orders for the Strangers' behaviour. Three articles were made concerning a particular institution created by the town authorities to oversee the good behaviour of the Strangers and to act as a link between the magistrates and the refugee community:

> Item that owte of your whoale companye, ye shalle electe & name to the maior for the tyme beinge, eight parsons for the Dutche congregation, and fower for the Wallownes, that shalbe governoures to the whoale companye and shalle take upon them the chardge and answeringe, for suche as shalbe fownde remysse and neclygente in parfourminge the articles afore (for Straungers) specifyed, or any article or order hereafter thought meete and necessary to be kept and observed.[4]

These eight and four should be elected annually and had to be presented to the Mayor for his approval. It is on this special institution known as the 'hommes politiques' or Politijcke Mannen that I would like to shed further light.

What were its particular functions and duties? How were they set down in accordance with both the church and the town authorities? Who were the men involved and how did they fit into the structure of the Norwich Dutch and Walloon Strangers' churches and into the religious theory and faith of the refugee communities in England?

Shortly after its foundation the Norwich Dutch community was shaken by internal conflicts between the three Dutch ministers Isbrandus Balkius, Carolus Ryckwaert and Antonius Algoet. In the course of these disputes the institution of the Politijcke Mannen was further developed, to a large extent according to the Dutch church elders' initiative. On the 24 February 1569 they presented twenty-four articles to the Mayor 'to mayntayne the churche here, in Chrystian peace and tranquilyte'.[5] Articles 12 to 15 set down the duties of the Politijcke Mannen and the procedure for their annual election.

---

[3] W.J.C. Moens, *The Walloons and their Church at Norwich*, vol.i, Lymington, 1887-8, p.25f

[4] NRO, DWSB, 17d, fol 19v

[5] NRO, DWSB, 17d, fol.39

They also defined what cases they should deal with, namely that they should

> mayntayne the ordenaunces appartayninge to the draperye and cangeauntrye ... And alle those politicalle matters whiche shalle come before them.⁶

The Book of Orders for Strangers, set down in 1571, further specified the duties of the Politijcke Mannen. They should act as 'arbitrators of pety cawse'⁷ between the community members. Moreover, after a request from the Dutch elders, the magistrates laid down that the Politijcke Mannen were exclusively responsible for the fulfilment of their orders. No English official should interfere in the Strangers' affairs except the Mayor, who had to be informed of their decisions.⁸

Dutch or Walloon documents relating to the formative phase of the Strangers' settlement in England are comparatively rare. A lively epistolary exchange between the London and the Norwich Dutch churches has survived, however, and suggests that the Politijcke Mannen were fully accepted as part of the social organisation of the immigrant community.⁹ The Politijcke Mannen were not only consulted by the church authorities on political and civil matters, but also took an active part in ecclesiastical decisions.¹⁰

Two documents set down by the Politijcke Mannen themselves further illuminate their duties and business in Norwich. The so-called *Norwich Strangers' Book*, a register running from April 1583 to June 1590 and with additions and notes from 1591 to 1600,¹¹ is mainly concerned with the guardianship of the orphans both of the Dutch and the French communities. At a time when at least one in three children had lost one parent by the age

---

⁶ NRO, DWSB, 17d, fol.40

⁷ NRO, DWSB, 17d, fol.48

⁸ NRO, DWSB, 17d, fol.75

⁹ *Ecclesiae Londino-Batavae Archivum*, ed. J.H. Hessels, Cambridge, 1889, vol.ii, nos. 304, 459

¹⁰ Hessels, *op.cit.*, vol.ii, no.904

¹¹ NRO, MC181/ms 2204

of fourteen[12] detailed provisions for the upbringing and education of orphans formed an essential part of the social organisation of every community. Each entry generally gives the name of the orphan or orphans concerned, the parents or other relatives, the names of the tutors, guarantors and other administrators. Also listed are the names of the Politijcke Mannen present at the meetings when the tutors had to declare the business done on behalf of their wards in the previous year. The notes were entered irregularly. Sometimes they were entered on a day-to-day basis, sometimes there are gaps of two months or more. They were written in Dutch or in French according to the language of the community concerned.

The second source of evidence is the *Book of the Norwich Dutch Church, 1605-1615*.[13] This is a minute book of the weekly meetings of the Politijcke Mannen. 'Ordinancien ghemaecht bij de onderschreven tot ouderlinghe eenichheit en vreede' - orders laid down in accordance with the elders - were set down and confirmed each year after the election of the twelve Politijcke Mannen which usually took place shortly after the election of the Mayor in the third week of June.

Again, the guardianship of orphans appears as one of their main tasks. But whereas in the older orphans' book, two or three Politijcke Mannen were sufficient to act on behalf of the whole committee, now decisions could be made only when all members were assembled. In addition this source shows that the Politijcke Mannen were also involved in the settlement of disputes between masters and apprentices, and between the governors of the Drapery and artisans who had offended against the rules and regulations of the trade.[14]

Politijcke Mannen frequently acted as testators or witnesses of testaments. They were asked to translate the last wills of their co-religionists from the French or Dutch original into English. In various cases they made or testified inventories of deceased members of the communities.[15]

---

[12] Lawrence Stone, *The Family, Sex and Marriage in England*, 1500-1800, abr.ed., Bungay, 1984, p.48

[13] BM Add. Ms 43, 862

[14] Book of the Norwich Dutch Church, fol.27, 28v, 59v, 81, 90v

[15] The inventory of Jacob Somerman is laid down in the Norwich Strangers' Book on the 3 April 1585, fol.24

THE *POLITIJCKE MANNEN*

By order of the Mayor the duties of the Politijcke Mannen were further enlarged on the 11 July 1573. They were now expected to examine all newcomers to the community and their guarantors before they were presented to the Mayor for approval.[16]

The case of Michiel Colens versus Remens van Rockeghems junior demonstrates how the Politijcke Mannen co-operated with the town authorities. In 1607 Michiel Colens had accused Remens van Rockeghems, tutor to his daughter Lydia, of unlawful dealings with Lydia's inheritance from her deceased mother. Van Rockeghems refused to lay open his accounts. The whole matter occupied the attention of the Politijcke Mannen for no less than eight years, since van Rockeghems was very inventive in finding various pretexts to hide his business.[17] Finally, on the 4 April 1615, he was sentenced to pay a fine of twenty shillings for his stubborn behaviour. He still refused to obey the orders of the Politijcke Mannen, however, and the whole affair was taken before the Mayor's Court, where the sentence was confirmed and van Rockeghems ordered to pay an additional twelve shillings for his disobedience. In the end the matter was settled when van Rockeghems paid the required amount on 18 July 1615, only three days after he had been sentenced by the Mayor's Court.[18]

This case is a good example of the way in which the Politijcke Mannen tried to deal with the city officials: with sheer dogged persistence in pursuing cases to a conclusion they tried to avoid the magistrates' interference for as long as possible.

It is interesting to note that they also dealt with the classic objects of Calvinistic disapproval: drunkenness, gaming and dancing. Quite a few Strangers were punished for scandalous talk or behaviour and for visits to public houses and cabarets.[19] It is difficult to decide which institution was regarded by the city authorities as the more competent in dealing with the affairs of the Strangers - the Politijcke Mannen or the elders of the churches -

---

[16] NRO, DWSB, 17d, fol.77v

[17] Several times he reported that everything had already been laid down at the Chancellor's Court. When the Politijcke Mannen insisted on seeing his bills, he asked Colens to go to the Continent and examine his business there.

[18] Book of the Norwich Dutch Church, fols 23, 23v, 116, 160, 165v; Mayor's Court Book, no.15, fol.22v

[19] Book of the Norwich Dutch Church, fol.42

especially as the Mayor sometimes addressed both the Politijcke Mannen and the elders of the churches with the same request.[20] The Court Book of the French Church, however, reveals that the Consistory was viewed both as the more prestigious and as the more influential committee among the Strangers.[21]

Who were these men that were chosen to act as Politijcke Mannen for the community? According to Article 12 of the twenty-four articles presented by the Dutch to the Mayor on the 24 February 1569, they were annually elected out of twenty-four persons, eight of whom had served as Politijcke Mannen in the previous year. The other sixteen candidates were chosen by the preachers, elders and deacons and by the governors of the Drapery. This system guaranteed a certain continuity in office-holding, but it is, nevertheless, remarkable how many of the names listed as members of the Politijcke Mannen also appear as elders and deacons. Looking at the various office-holders in the communities it is clear that the government of the Strangers was dominated by a small clique of influential families - mainly from a merchant background - like the Bonnells, the Desbonnets and the Wallwyns.

How can the institution of the Politijcke Mannen in Norwich be interpreted in the context of the religious and social network of the other refugee communities in England?

As has been shown, their organisation was born out of the particular circumstances in the city. One important feature was the strong and influential city magistracy in Norwich eager to keep the costs of the newcomers for the city as low as possible, and at the same time keen to have a guarantee for the well-ordered, quiet behaviour of the Strangers. The local authorities must have become uneasy when faced with the internal disputes in the Strangers' churches on the one hand and the unexpected and unorganised influx of refugees who could not be controlled solely by church discipline on the other. In these particular circumstances, both the town authorities and the church elders invented and developed the institution of the Politijcke Mannen as a civil branch of the church administration.

The idea of a permanent secular branch to deal with Strangers' affairs was observed with interest by the other refugee communities in England and

---

[20] Mayor's Court Book, no.11, fols 407v, 473

[21] NRO, Actes du Consistoire de L'Église Wallonne de Norwich, 31, G, fols 44-7

regarded as an acceptable method of settling disputes. The Consistory of the French church in Canterbury, for example, declared on the 25 July 1576 that it did not feel responsible for civil and political matters.[22] These matters were at first referred to arbitrators, but from 1582 onwards the church created the institution of Politijcke Mannen with duties similar to the ones in Norwich, that is supervision of newcomers and punishment of civil misbehaviour.[23] The distinction between civil and ecclesiastical jurisdiction was formally laid down at the Colloquy of the French refugee churches assembled in 1582.[24]

The idea of submission under worldly orders was part of the Strangers' churches' religious theory that was more strongly influenced by Zwingli's concept of church organisation than by the strict Calvinistic faith characteristic of the churches in the Netherlands. According to the Zurich version of church organisation, discipline and rites were regarded as *a diaphora*, which means their substance and form could be left to the decisions of secular authorities. Worldly and ecclesiastical officials were not interchangeable but coexistent. Each body had its particular functions and duties in a God-given social organisation. The maintenance of godly and well-ordered behaviour among the members of a community was ultimately a matter for the church, but it could be handed over to the respective civil authorities as long as they obeyed God's orders.

The adoption of such Zwinglian concepts by the refugee churches in England was to a great extent motivated by à Lasco himself who was strongly influenced by the example of Zurich. In addition, the refugees had to pay regard to the religious situation in their host communities. Fortunately for the newcomers there was a consensus in matters of faith and doctrines between the refugee churches and the Anglican confession. Differences occurred mainly over certain aspects of rites and church orders. With the acceptance of the cryptoepiscopal office of a superintendent in the person of the Bishop of Norwich, and of the town magistrates' ultimate supervision over the Strangers' civil affairs, the church elders agreed to a viable compromise between their own autonomy as a self-sufficient

---

[22] Canterbury Cathedral Archive, U47 A1/14r, Actes du Consistoire, 1576-8

[23] U47 A2/7, Actes du Consistoire, 1581-4

[24] *Les Actes des Colloques des Églises Françaises et des Synodes des Églises Étrangères réfugiées en Angleterre, 1581-1654*, ed. Adrian Charles Chaumier, Lymington, 1890

ecclesiastical and social body within their host community and the magistrates' desire to control and supervise their activities within the framework of the city organisation.

As we have seen, the institution of the Politijcke Mannen formed an essential part of this mutual agreement and helped to maintain a peaceful and quiet social life both for the Strangers and for the indigenous population in England's second city.

PUBLICATIONS CONNECTED WITH THE DUTCH CHURCH IN NORWICH

WILLIAM J. WOODS

About 5,000 refugees from the Spanish conquest of the Netherlands settled in Norwich during the latter half of the sixteenth century, eventually making up almost a third of the population of the city. They were called the 'Strangers' and consisted of a majority Dutch and Flemish community referred to as the Dutch, and a minority French-speaking community referred to as the Walloons. Their principal trade was weaving and they were helped by the Corporation and Diocese who provided them with premises for a cloth hall and a church. The Dutch church in Norwich opened in December 1565 and before long others had been established in Yarmouth, King's Lynn and Thetford. Only the churches at Norwich and Yarmouth lasted for more than a few years: that at Norwich was large and lasted for more than three centuries. One of the ministers, Elison, and his wife, born and bred locally, have the distinction of having been painted by Rembrandt.

Although most of the Strangers were weavers, a variety of other trades were recorded among them and one of these was printing. The first printing-press ever established in Norwich was a Dutch press which operated between 1568 and 1572. Printing was not undertaken again in Norwich for more than a hundred years. Anthony de Solemne, the printer, came to Norwich from Antwerp in 1567 and his press was established in the parish of St Andrew's, close to the Dutch church which stood on one side of St Andrew's Plain. Solemne was recorded as being a spice merchant in Antwerp. Later in Norwich he was described as a printer and wine merchant, and three of the surviving works from his press state merely that they were printed at his house, so he may principally have been the proprietor and had others doing the actual work.

Six publications survive from Solemne's press, three more publications exist with attributions to the Dutch press in Norwich which are false, and one further publication connected with the Dutch church in Norwich was printed in Amsterdam. Of the six works genuinely printed on Solemne's press, four are religious works and two are of a secular nature; three are in Dutch, two in English and one in French. The three Dutch works are books, two religious and one secular; the other works are broadsheets, one religious in French, one secular and one religious in English. The high quality printing and binding of the Dutch books, combined with the fact that the Norwich press had a reputation in the Netherlands which led to publications printed there spuriously being attributed to Norwich, suggest that much of the output in Dutch was exported back to the Low Countries and even that the press was set up with a view as much to producing works for export as to satisfying local consumption. Some of the publications of Solemne have been found together with, and even bound with, publications of a similar Dutch refugee press in Emden, that of William Gailliart. Solemne's type-faces are quite similar to those of Gailliart and probably came from the same source. There seem to have been good communications between Dutch refugee communities, notably those in Norwich, Emden and London.

Solemne is recorded in 1570 as having been used by Norwich Corporation to print bye-laws and by St Andrew's parish to print proclamations. Only the first two books, published in 1568, are specifically for the Dutch church. After this date there is a reduction in scale from books to broadsheets and a diversification of subject matter from Dutch religious texts to other customer commissions. This was accompanied by a narrowing of the market from the Dutch church in Europe to a little local trade and, after only four years, the press closed down. However, the repercussions of this short period of Dutch printing activity in Norwich lasted to the middle of the next century. An annotated list of the ten surviving works of varying connection with the Dutch church in Norwich follows:[1]

1. *De C.L. Psalmen Dauids.* 1568
   TOT NOORWITZ Gheprint by Anthonium de Solemne

'The 150 Psalms of David'. Translated from French verse into Dutch by

---

[1] William Sessions and David Stoker, *The First Printers in Norwich from 1567 - Anthony de Solempne, Albert Christiaensz and Johannes Paetz*, York, 1987 provides much information on the first eight works

Petrus Dathenus. Music with words underneath. Each psalm is preceded by a summary of its content and followed by a prayer. To the right of the musical text stands the literal Dutch Bible text. The whole is preceded by an introduction on the fundamentals of psalm music and is followed by a catechism. This version of the psalms was first published in Flanders in 1556 and became popular in the Dutch church. The London church, which had a different version printed in 1566, switched to the Dathenus version in 1571, three years after it had appeared in Norwich.

2. *Belijdenisse ende eenvoudige wtlegghinge des waerachtigen gheloofs/ ende der algemeynen articulen van de suyuere Christelicke religie/* ... 1568 Gheprint tot Nordwitz by Antonium de Solemne

'Confession and simple explanation of the true faith/ and of the general articles of the pure Christian religion/ ...'. This is an edition of the popular so-called 'Helvetic Confessions' and carries a heading across each pair of facing pages stating that it is the confession of faith of the churches of Switzerland.

3. *Tableau de l'oeuure de Dieu.* 1569

No attribution of printing. Single broadsheet tabling works of God in paragraphs condensed from the Bible by Antonio del Corro, a preacher of the refugee Spanish congregation in London. Commissioned by Corro from Solemne and a cause of some dispute in London, as explained by John Strype in 1710:

> Corranus of late hath caused a Table, entitled De Operibus Dei, wrote by him in French, to be Printed in Norwich, not offering the same to be Examined here before it was printed. But the Minister and Seniors of the Italian Church, had misliked certain Doctrines contained in the said Table, wavering, as it seems, somewhat from the opinions of Calvin.[2]

Solemne got into difficulties with the minister of the Walloon church in Norwich to whom he showed the proofs for correction of the French. The

---

[2] John Strype, *Biography of Edmund Grindal*, 1710, p.125

Minister, De la Forest, covered the margins with twenty-five censures claiming that the Tableau attacked orthodox Christology and predestination. Solemne, nevertheless, went ahead and printed the broadsheet and the outcome for Corro was his suspension by Bishop Grindal from preaching or reading. Corro explained that he had had the Tableau printed in Norwich because Anthony de Solemne could quote the lowest price. Solemne was prepared to run off an edition of 100 copies for a crown, whereas London printers would only do a minimum of 1500 copies. Copies of the Tableau in French and Latin printed elsewhere in the following year also survive.

4. *Certayne versis/ writtene by Thomas Brooke Gētleman/ in the tyme of his imprisōment the daye before his deathe/ who sufferyd at Norwich/ the 30. of August 1570*
Imprynted at Norwich in the Paryshe of Saynct Andrewes/ by Anthony de Solemne. 1570

After his previous rogue effort, which may have earned him some official reprimand, Solemne is careful to state at the end of this text that it was 'Seane/ and allowyd accordynge to the Quenes Maiestyes Iniunction. God save the Quene'. The verses are of a conciliatory nature, from a man making peace with God preparatory to execution. Ironically Brooke was hanged at Norwich Castle for being one of the leaders of an uprising in May and June 1570, the aim of which was to drive the Strangers out of Norwich. The cause of the conspiracy was not religious, but material jealousy among the native population. Queen Elizabeth reacted to the uprising with a letter written from the Palace at Greenwich dated 19 March 1570. She reminded the citizens of Norwich of the advantages they had derived from the settlement amongst them of so many skilled workers who inhabited houses which previously had been standing empty, and who provided work for large numbers of people who would otherwise have been unemployed. She therefore entreated them to continue their favours 'to the poor men of the Dutch nation, who seeing the persecution lately begun in their country for the true religion, have fled into this realm for succour, and were now placed in the city of Norwich'.[3] The Strangers had originally come at the

---

[3] A.D. Bayne, *Royal Illustrated History of Eastern England*, Great Yarmouth, 1873, p.117

instigation of the Mayor and sheriffs who had persuaded the Duke of Norfolk to use his influence to induce a detachment of refugee Dutch and Walloon families to settle in Norwich at his charge and to carry on their trades under a licence granted by the Queen. The 1570 conspiracy was, therefore, directly in conflict with the Duke of Norfolk and the Queen. Three leaders were hanged.

5. *EENEN Calendier historiael/ eewelick gheduerende.* 1570
   Ghedruct tot Noorwitz/ ten huyse van Anthonium de Solemne

'A Calendar historical/ everlasting'. Sixteen-page booklet including times of sunrise and sunset and annual fairs in various countries. Although secular, such universal calendars preface some editions of the New Testament and the Bible. It notes the date on which Queen Elizabeth decreed that the Strangers might settle in Norwich and records that the Dutch church opened there on 24 December 1565.

6. *A Prayer to be sayd in the end of mornyng prayer daily (through the dioeces of Norwich) during the tyme of this hard and sharp wether/ of frost and snow/ to craue mercye for our synnes/ and release of this sore punishment at the mercifull handes of our good and graciouse God.* 1572
   Imprinted at Norwich in ye parish of St Andrewe by Antho: de Solempne

This broadsheet is the last surviving genuine product of the Dutch press in Norwich, evidently a Church of England commission and an indication of good relations between the immigrant community and the established church.

7. *Het tweede boeck, Vande sermoenen des wel vermaerden Predicants B. Cornelis Adriaenssen van Dordrecht/ Minrebroeder tot Brugge.* 1578
   Nu eerstmael in Druck vuytgegeven, buyten Noirdwitz

'The second book, Of the sermons of the truly celebrated Priest B. Cornelis Adriaenssen of Dordrecht/Minorite at Bruges'. The place of printing is claimed to be 'outside Norwich', but this is implausible for several reasons. No evidence exists for any press operating in the vicinity of Norwich at this time and although the work is in Dutch, the type-faces are unlike those of Solemne's printing-press. Adriaenssen was an extremist Catholic preacher and these sermons are a forgery in his name, full of vulgarity and meant to parody and denigrate him. They have no relevance to the Dutch community in Norwich except in being anti-Catholic. It is possible that the first book of his sermons of 1569, also a forgery, was printed in Norwich and the place used as an attribution for the second book. This attribution is a red herring, probably intended to protect the identity of the printer in a local Flemish religious conflict. Reference to Norwich does, however, show how far the City's reputation for printing Dutch dissenting works had spread.

8. *CHRONYC. Historie der Nederlandtscher Oorlogen/ Troublen en oproeren oorspronck/ anvanck en eynde/ Item den Standt der Religien/ tot desen Jar 1580*
Gedruct tot Noortwitz na de Copie van Basel. Anno 1579

'CHRONICLE. History of the origin/ start and end of the Dutch Wars/ Troubles and disturbances/ Likewise the Position of Religion/ up to this year 1580'. By Adam Henricipetri of Basle. The date of printing is given as 1579 despite the year stated in the title. The book is said to be printed according to the copy of Basle and the place of printing is claimed to be Norwich, but the type-faces are not consistent with Solemne's. Once again the false reference to Norwich was probably intended to protect the printer and distributors of controversial religious material in the Netherlands. The Chronicle gives daily details from a Protestant viewpoint of troubles and sufferings under Catholic persecution.

9. *Uytbreydinge over den Achtsten Psalm Davids.* 1642
Amsterdam

'Expansion on the Eighth Psalm of David' by Jan Cruso, who was a captain of the Strangers' militia in Norwich and an elder of the Dutch church there. Cruso wrote a number of works in English on military subjects for the English market and two volumes of Dutch poetry published in Holland, both of which make reference to Norwich. His expansion on the eighth psalm is appropriate in view of the publication of the psalms in Dutch in Norwich in the previous century. The verse text is said to be based on work by a sixteenth-century French Protestant poet, Du Bartas, but Cruso does include lines about his home territory around Norwich including the River Yare, which seems to be the first original Norfolk poetry in Dutch. In translated version it runs:

> Yes while I this describe
> and in green dales
> I walk beside the Yare
> to take a little air
> and to the city
> through thick woods do turn,
> How I am there regaled
> By the choir of Nightingales!

At the back of the book is printed a lament for John Elison, who was minister of the Dutch church in Norwich from 1603 to 1639, with an inscription that it is an elegy on the untimely death of the most learned and devout Revd IOANNES ELISONIUS, 'Getrou Bedienaer der Neder-Duytsche Gemeynte CHRISTI in NORWITS' [Faithful Servant of the Dutch Community of CHRIST in NORWICH].

10. *MUNDUS VULT DECIPI*
   Geprent te Norwitse
   Bachtent de Duutsche kercke, in Leviatan,
   Dat de Eere em stercke, tegen Prins Robbrecht en Satan

The translation of the Latin title is 'The World wants to be deceived'. Undated but circa 1644. Attributed to Vondel, the leading Dutch poet and playwright. Twenty-eight-line poem in rhyming couplets in the style of a satire. No original broadsheet exists, the earliest surviving copy being in a book of Vondel's poetry published in 1647. Attribution to Vondel and two references to Norwich are all false.[4] The satire is political, but with religious undertones. Firstly it describes how a certain Sir Thomas of Norwich was suffering from toothache, to cure which a Master Scott, lodging in Newcastle, was summoned who pulled out his tooth and with it his whole jawbone. The 'Sir Thomas' referred to is Sir Thomas Fairfax, commander-in-chief of the Parliamentarian army in the Civil War, who had no connection with Norwich although the city was in a predominantly Parliamentarian

---

[4] William J. Woods, 'The World was Deceived': on 'Mundus Vult Decipi' attributed to Vondel' in *Dutch Crossing*, 10, March 1980, p.25-35

region. Secondly it is stated underneath the poem that it was printed at Norwich and there follows a rhyming couplet which translates as:

Behind the Dutch church, in Leviathan,
That the Lord strengthen himself, against Prince Robbrecht and Satan

Robbrecht is Dutch for Rupert, cavalry commander of the Royalist forces and tolerant towards Roman Catholics. The poet has, therefore, chosen to specify Norwich because of its Dutch church and general anti-Catholic orientation. Vondel, of Flemish Protestant parentage, had settled in Amsterdam, had converted to Roman Catholicism in his fifties in 1641 and staunchly supported the Royalist cause in the English Civil War. This bogus satire in an exaggeratedly Flemish style of language is intended to mock both Vondel and political bargaining in the Civil War. Amsterdam may have become more aware of Norwich around this time because the Reverend Elison and his wife visited Amsterdam in 1634 and had their portraits painted by Rembrandt and because Jan Cruso, also of the Dutch church, published his volume of poetry in Amsterdam in 1642. 'Mundus Vult Decipi' was probably written in 1644 after Scottish forces occupied Newcastle as a result of the 'Solemn League and Covenant' of 1643, whereby Scottish Presbyterian assistance was offered to the Roundheads in return for Anglican church reform and the eradication of popery. The deal is here mocked as an outrageous concession to the Scots. Although Vondel did write satires and did concern himself with English politics, the anti-Royalist footnote could not be his trademark. In fact the Dutch community in Norwich kept a low profile during the Civil War because, although opposed to Catholicism, they were also indebted to royal favour. While their printing-press was in operation there is no sign that they allowed it to be used for any English religious agitation. Continued involvement in religious controversy abroad seems to have been balanced, regardless of other local disputes, by good relations with the ecclesiastic authorities at home.

EVIDENCE FOR DISSENT IN NORFOLK 1711-1800 FROM THE RECORDS OF THE DIOCESE OF NORWICH

W.M. JACOB

The Toleration Act of 1689 permitted Protestant Dissenters to legalise their meeting-houses as alternatives to parish churches by registering and certifying them with the Bishop's registrar or with the Clerk of Justices in Quarter Sessions. Among the records of the Diocese of Norwich a list of certificates for meeting-houses issued between 1711 and 1721 survives, together with a register of meeting-houses certified between 1751-1811.[1] This paper is based on the evidence of these sources.

The information provided by the first of these sources is limited to the year, the name of the applicant, the name of the owner of the property to be registered, and the name of the place in which it lies. The second source, the Register, gives merely the date, the name of the applicant and, occasionally, some indication of the premises and of the sect for whose use they were to be registered.

Considering first the earlier period, during the twelve years covered by the list, fifty-four buildings were registered as meeting-houses. The largest number was registered in 1712 (eleven) followed by 1711 (seven), 1715 (seven) and 1718 (six). In 1717 only one building was registered. The fifty-four buildings were in thirty-six places (discounting Norwich for which there were four certificates in three parishes: St James, St Paul and St Giles). Their geographical distribution is of interest. Five are in Great Yarmouth, three in King's Lynn and there is also a scattering in the hinterlands of these towns - for Filby in 1717, West Walton in 1711 and for Ashwicken in 1716. Apart from these, there are clusters of applications from the south of the county around the Pulhams, Harleston, Diss, Winfarthing and Kenninghall; from the area around North Walsham, Smallburgh and Barton Turf in the north-

---

[1] NRO, DIS/1

east; and from the district around Saxthorpe, Corpusty and Oulton in central Norfolk. In addition, there are single applications for Wymondham, Mattishall, Breccles, Weeting and Southery.

Often the same applicants crop up more than once. For example in 1711 Daniel Killingworth sought licences for properties in North Walsham, Smallburgh and Thorpe-next-Norwich, in 1714 for Swanton Abbott and in 1716 for Honing. Thomas Allen applied for licences for properties in Wymondham and Great Yarmouth in 1712, and for Dickleburgh and Pulham St Mary Magdalen in 1713, while Abraham Moore registered a house in Friary Yard, St James' Norwich in 1712 and houses in Pulham Market and Weeting in 1714. John Dunthorne owned a house which was registered in Dickleburgh in 1713. He registered a property in Diss in 1715 and in 1718 properties in Winfarthing and Pulham St Mary Magdalen.

Of the fifty-four premises registered, six were owned by women - Ann Roberts at Thorpe-next-Norwich in 1711, Ann Taylor at Pulham Market in 1714, Margaret Wright at Redenhall in 1715, Ann Clarke at Harleston in 1718, Widow Davy at Kenninghall in 1719 and Mary Fisher at Corpusty in 1720.

There is no indication of the sects to which these people belonged. Browne notes Independent meeting-houses at Wymondham (1652), Tunstead (1652) Bradfield (1660), Guestwick (1652), Oulton (1730), Lynn (1662) Harleston (1708) and Mattishall (early eighteenth century[2]), and a Presbyterian chapel-at-ease to Yarmouth at Filby in 1717.[3] Jewson notes a Grantham Killingworth as a grandson of Thomas Grantham who introduced Arminian Baptist doctrine to Norfolk from Lincolnshire in the 1680s, and the name is sufficiently uncommon to suspect a kinship with the Daniel Killingworth active in north-east Norfolk.[4] Jewson also notes the existence of Baptist meeting-houses at Smallburgh, Worstead and Tibenham,[5] all of which are in areas of high licensing activity. Browne similarly noted a Baptist

---

[2] John Browne, *History of Congregationalism and Memorials of the Churches in Norfolk and Suffolk*, 1877, pp.289-351

[3] Browne, *ibid.*, p.365

[4] C.B. Jewson, *The Baptists in Norfolk*, 1957, p.29

[5] Jewson, *ibid.*, p.46-54

church at Pulham in 1713.[6]

The marked tendency for applications to cluster in particular localities raises the question of why Dissent was active in some areas and not in others. Michael Watts has suggested that Dissent was a predominantly urban phenomenon in the early eighteenth century,[7] that Independents and Particular Baptists were strongest in areas where Puritanism had been strong in the previous century and that in Wiltshire the Particular Baptists were especially strong in the textile manufacturing areas.[8] These observations, especially the second and third, may have some relevance to Norfolk. However, unless evidence of significantly more Dissenting activity is yet to be discovered in the records of the Clerks to the Justices it would seem that Dissent was numerically a very modest affair in the county in this period.[9]

The later period for which the Diocesan records produce evidence - 1751 to 1811 - shows the slow emergence of a different picture. Until 1770 there is little increase in the rate of registration. Between 1751 and 1760, fifty-two properties are registered (two fewer than in 1711-20) and in the 1760s there is a sharp drop to a mere thirty-four properties. Between 1771 and 1780, however, there is a strong increase to eighty-six; in the period 1781 to 1790 there is a slight fall back to seventy-three; but then from 1791 to 1800, no less then 173 properties are registered. Significantly, the third entry in the register is an application by James Wheatley who, being reconciled to John Wesley after an earlier doctrinal and disciplinary breach, began preaching in Norwich in 1751.[10]

Of the 418 properties registered between 1751 and 1800 only thirty-seven are described as chapels or meeting-houses. It is clear that some, at least, originally had another function. Examples include the Foundry in St Stephen's Norwich in 1755, the Malthouse in St Paul's Norwich in 1756, the

---

[6] Browne, *op.cit.*, p.549

[7] M.R. Watts, *The Dissenters from the Reformation to the French Revolution*, Oxford, 1978, p.285

[8] Watts, *ibid.*, p.282

[9] Watts, *ibid.*, p.270 suggests that in the early eighteenth century, Dissenters amounted to 6.21% of the population

[10] Cyril Jolly, *The Spreading Flame: The Coming of Methodism to Norfolk 1751-1811*, privately printed, no date

Old Playhouse in St Peter Mancroft and a 'warehouse' in St James's Norwich in 1758. A number are described as 'a barn' or, as at North Lopham in 1788, 'a barn fitted up'. From 1798 the property registered is often described as 'a school room'. The majority, however, are not described; probably they were simply rooms in cottages or houses. At Brandon Parva in 1768 Samuel Pettingale registered 'Barbary Dobson's Kitchen'; some kitchens may have been smarter than others, however, for in 1780 Joseph Robins registered 'the kitchen of Irmingland Hall'. Outbuildings attached to inns were not despised; in 1780 the barn at the Feathers at Holt was registered. In 1781 John Hunt, Surgeon of St John de Sepulchre, Norwich, even registered his summer-house.

Of the 316 properties, eighty-seven were in eight towns - thirty-three in Norwich, ten in Wymondham, ten in Lynn (in two parishes), nine in East Dereham, eight in Great Yarmouth, seven in Diss, six in Loddon and four in Fakenham. The remaining 229 were in 200 parishes. By 1800, therefore, only about a third of Norfolk parishes had a property registered for Dissenting worship. Obviously, people wishing to attend a Dissenting place of worship might have been willing to travel some distance.[11] Nevertheless, only 287 out of 579 returns by clergy to the Bishop's Visitation Inquiries in 1784 mention Dissenters living in the parish. Even in 1806, only 297 out of 685 returns noted Dissenters. These comparatively low figures may represent a lack of information, or the clergy's reluctance to impart this knowledge to the bishops. It may mean, however, that in general those places which lacked a meeting-place also lacked Dissenters.[12] In some instances omission may have been due to problems of definition. In 1777 the incumbent of Titchwell, where a property had been registered for Dissenting worship in 1775 by a very energetic Methodist preacher, doubted whether he should mention Methodists as Dissenters.[13]

Again, there are strong geographical concentrations of registrations. They

---

[11] Margaret Spufford, *Contrasting Communities: English Villagers in the Sixteenth and Seventeenth Centuries*, Cambridge, 1974, p.346 ff. suggests that growth of Dissent split communities and households on ideological grounds and shows how people travelled to chapels in towns and larger villages

[12] W.M. Jacob, Church and Society in Norfolk 1707-1806, unpublished PhD thesis, University of Exeter, 1982, p.411

[13] *Ibid.*, p.417

are particularly numerous in south Norfolk, especially in the area running south from Wymondham to the county boundary; in the districts to the south-east and north-east of Norwich; in central Norfolk between Barford and Dereham; in the triangle of country between Fakenham, Burnham Market and Holt; and around Lynn and Downham Market. There are relatively few in the areas to the west of Dereham, or in north-west Norfolk.

As in the earlier source, some names appear as applicants more than once. Twenty-one people registered more than one property, but of these, fourteen registered only two. Some operated in limited geographical areas: William Denton of Walsingham registered properties in Sharrington and Burnham Overy in 1793 and 'a chapel' in New Walsingham in 1794. Others operated over wide areas: George Shadford registered properties at Great Yarmouth, Loddon and King's Lynn, all in 1772. John Perowne registered properties at Great Ellingham, King's Lynn and Winfarthing, all in 1773; Samuel Bardsey of Norwich registered a property at Honing in 1779 and at 'Hitcham', Haddiscoe and North Lopham in 1780. The most active were Francis Osborn who registered properties at Wacton and 'Bareham' in 1758, 'Brundale' in 1759, Burston and Forncett St Peter in 1760 and Tibenham in 1766 and Thomas Mendham who registered properties in Hunworth in 1774, Wells, Titchwell, Great Ryburgh and Colkirk in 1775, South Creake in 1779, Titchwell again and Downham Market in 1780 and Docking in 1781. It seems that people were active as applicants over relatively short periods of time, mostly over only one or two years. Even Mendham and Osborn were only active during seven- or eight-year periods.

Fourteen of the applicants are noted as 'religious designated professionals', that is, they were designated as 'Dissenting Minister', 'Preacher', 'Minister of the Gospel', 'Itinerant Preacher', or 'Dissenting teacher of the Gospel'. In only one case, however, is a denomination indicated; Daniel Walters, who registered the Old Quaker Meeting House in King's Lynn in 1779, is noted as an 'Independent Preacher'.

In many instances, the applicants' occupation is recorded. In general these represent the middling and artisan ranks of society. There are a large number of tradesmen and craftsmen, but the biggest occupational group represented are farmers of whom there are no less than thirty-nine. They, together with eighteen husbandmen, six yeomen and five millers suggest that Dissent was a significant phenomenon among the middle ranks of rural society. There are also twenty-six applicants engaged in the textile industry, five woolcombers, twelve worsted weavers, nine cordwainers. However, these too may have been rural occupations. It is also notable that there were seven gentlemen among the applicants as well as eighteen labourers. Another socially significant group were schoolmasters, of whom eight appear as applicants.

There are fewer women among the applicants than earlier in the century; only four (and a joint application by a husband and wife or a sister and brother) between 1751 and 1790, and only eleven (out of a total of 173 applicants) between 1791 and 1800. One might have expected more, given John Wesley's fairly positive attitude towards women in his societies[14] and the participation of women in active leadership roles in Methodist societies in Leeds[15] and Cheshire.[16] This may be an indication of the reduction in opportunities for leadership for women even in Dissenting bodies in the late eighteenth century.[17] However, to demonstrate the limitations of the evidence from the register, John Browne records that in 1799 two 'maiden ladies' named Glover built a chapel at South Creake to hold 250 and added 'It is said they conducted services there themselves for some time'.[18] The register does not mention this, unless they used the 'meeting-house' registered by Thomas Mendham at South Creake in 1779.

A few of the properties registered are identified with a particular Dissenting sect. The register mentions an 'Anabaptist' meeting-house at Ingham in 1764, the New Quaker meeting-house at Lynn in 1775 (registered by Joseph Peckover), an Independent chapel in the Old Quaker meeting-house in Lynn in 1779, the Methodist chapel at Briston in 1783, and a Methodist meeting-house at East Dereham in 1788. Methodists also licensed properties in Norton [Subcourse] in 1790 and Wellingham in 1791. An Independent meeting-house was registered at Wymondham in 1791, a Baptist meeting-house at Great Ellingham in 1792 and Methodists registered a chapel at Great Yarmouth in 1792 and at Downham Market in 1793. A property

---

[14] Earl Kent Brown, *Women of Mr Wesley's Methodism*, Lewiston, New York, 1983

[15] D. Colin Dews, 'Ann Carr and the Female Revivalists of Leeds' in *Religion in the Lives of English Women 1760-1930*, ed. Gail Malmgreen, 1986

[16] Gail Malmgreen, 'Domestic Discords, Women and the Family in East Cheshire Methodism, 1750-1830', in *Disciplines of Faith*, ed. Jim Obelkevich, Lyndal Roper and Raphael Samuel, 1987

[17] Leonore Davidoff and Catherine Hall, *Family Fortunes*, 1987, p.137 ff

[18] Browne, *op.cit.*, p.363

called 'The Baptistry' was registered at Fersfield in 1795; Methodist chapels at North Walsham in 1797, at East Harling, Holme Hale and Needham in 1798; and, also in 1798, a Quaker meeting-house at East Harling. Methodist chapels were registered at Thorpe-next-Haddiscoe, Lingwood, Great Yarmouth and Cley in 1799; Baptists registered meeting-houses at Pulham St Mary Magdalen in the same year and at Martham and Gissing in 1800. For the rest there is no clear designation.

It may be possible to identify some individuals and buildings from denominational records. However, this is more complicated than it looks. The denominational histories can be of some assistance. For instance, Cyril Jolly identifies George Shadford as one of Wesley's preachers in Norwich from 1770-2 and he registered properties at Great Yarmouth, Loddon and King's Lynn in 1772. John Perowne provided the site for Wesley's Cherry Lane chapel in Norwich in 1769, and he registered properties in Great Ellingham, King's Lynn and Winfarthing in 1773. Joseph Pilmoor was a Methodist preacher in Norwich in 1777 and registered a property at Northwold in 1779.[19] Browne and Jewson list a number of places where they have evidence of Independent and Baptist meeting-houses and the names of ministers. However, Jewson's list at least is clearly not exhaustive. Thus the register notes properties at Fersfield and Gissing as being registered by Baptists, but Jewson makes no mention of these.

One difficulty is that people moved between sects. Mark Wilks, for example, began his ministerial career in Norwich as a Calvinistic Methodist in Lady Huntingdon's Connexion. He was Minister at the Tabernacle, a building which had originally been registered by James Wheatley, who had quarrelled with John Wesley. Wheatley subsequently made over his interest to Wesley who, when he preached there in 1759, noted that a considerable part of the congregation were Dissenters. In 1765 Wesley relinquished his interest in the Tabernacle to John Hook, who managed it on James Wheatley's behalf. In April 1776 negotiations were concluded for Lady Huntingdon to lease the building for £40 per annum. In 1776 she bought Wheatley's share in the building for £500. She had installed Mark Wilks there, but expelled him in 1778 when he married. Some of the congregation seceded with Wilks, bought a chapel in Norwich that had originally been built by Thomas Bowman the evangelical vicar of Martham, and invited

---

[19] Jolly, *op.cit.*, pp.24-5

Wilks to preach there. At first the congregation remained Calvinistic Methodist, (though out of connexion with Lady Huntingdon) but it subsequently became Baptist.[20] This may be an extreme case, but it does illustrate the tendency for buildings to change hands between different Dissenting groups, for individuals to move from one group to another, and for congregations to change denomination.

The second half of the eighteenth century saw a general religious revival which affected both the established church and the old Dissenting denominations. This created a variety of new groups, of which John Wesley's was only one (but the best organised). The activities of Wesley and his preachers and the revival of the Old Dissenting congregations by no means account for all the meeting-houses licensed in Norfolk during the last thirty years of the eighteenth century. It is probably impossible to identify the theological complexion of the majority of those who licensed meeting-houses in this period. Many probably belonged to no organised society or connexion but were part of a general uprising of Dissenting and protesting radical religious groups which, at a later date, provided a fertile soil for Primitive Methodism. Clergy of the established church were also caught up in this movement. The vicar of Martham, Thomas Bowman, who in 1768 had built the chapel in Norwich later bought by Wilks' seceding congregation, had earlier, in 1766, established a congregation in Cawston in rivalry to the parish church. He continued to minister to this chapel until his death in 1792.[21]

In the last thirty years of the eighteenth century there was an upsurge of religious expression which could not be contained either by the Church of England or by the existing Dissenting groups. The Norfolk evidence indicates that it was not merely an urban or industrial phenomenon. Further questions requiring exploration are why some places rather than others had Dissenting congregations. It would, in particular, be interesting to know whether they had witnessed earlier Puritan activity; whether charity or endowed schools had been established there earlier in the century; and whether they were 'open' or 'closed' parishes. Further research should be directed towards discovering whether there were any ecclesiastical,

---

[20] Browne, *op.cit*, pp.189-97. For Wilkes' subsequent career as a radical politician in Norwich see C.B. Jewson, *Jacobin City*, Glasgow & London, 1975

[21] R.W. Ketton Cremer, *Forty Norfolk Essays*, Norwich, 1961, pp.65-7

demographic, geographical or economic factors which were shared by the relevant parishes[22] - for instance, whether they had a resident incumbent, whether the incumbent was a JP, whether there had been recent enclosure on a significant scale. It would also be valuable to investigate possible correlations between the incidence of social protest in parishes in the last decade of the eighteenth century and the occurrence of Dissenting meeting-places.[23]

---

[22] e.g. Alan Everitt, *The Pattern of Rural Dissent; The 19th Century*, Leicester, 1972

[23] How might this relate to E.P., Thompson's theories in *The Making of the English Working Class*, 1968 and the research in A.J. Peacock, *Bread or Blood: The Agrarian Riots in East Anglia 1816*, 1965 and E.J. Hobsbawm and G. Rudé, *Captain Swing*, 1973? Surprisingly no reference whatsoever is made to religious Dissent in *Class Conflict and Protest in the English Countryside 1700-1880*, eds Mick Reed and Roger Wells, 1990

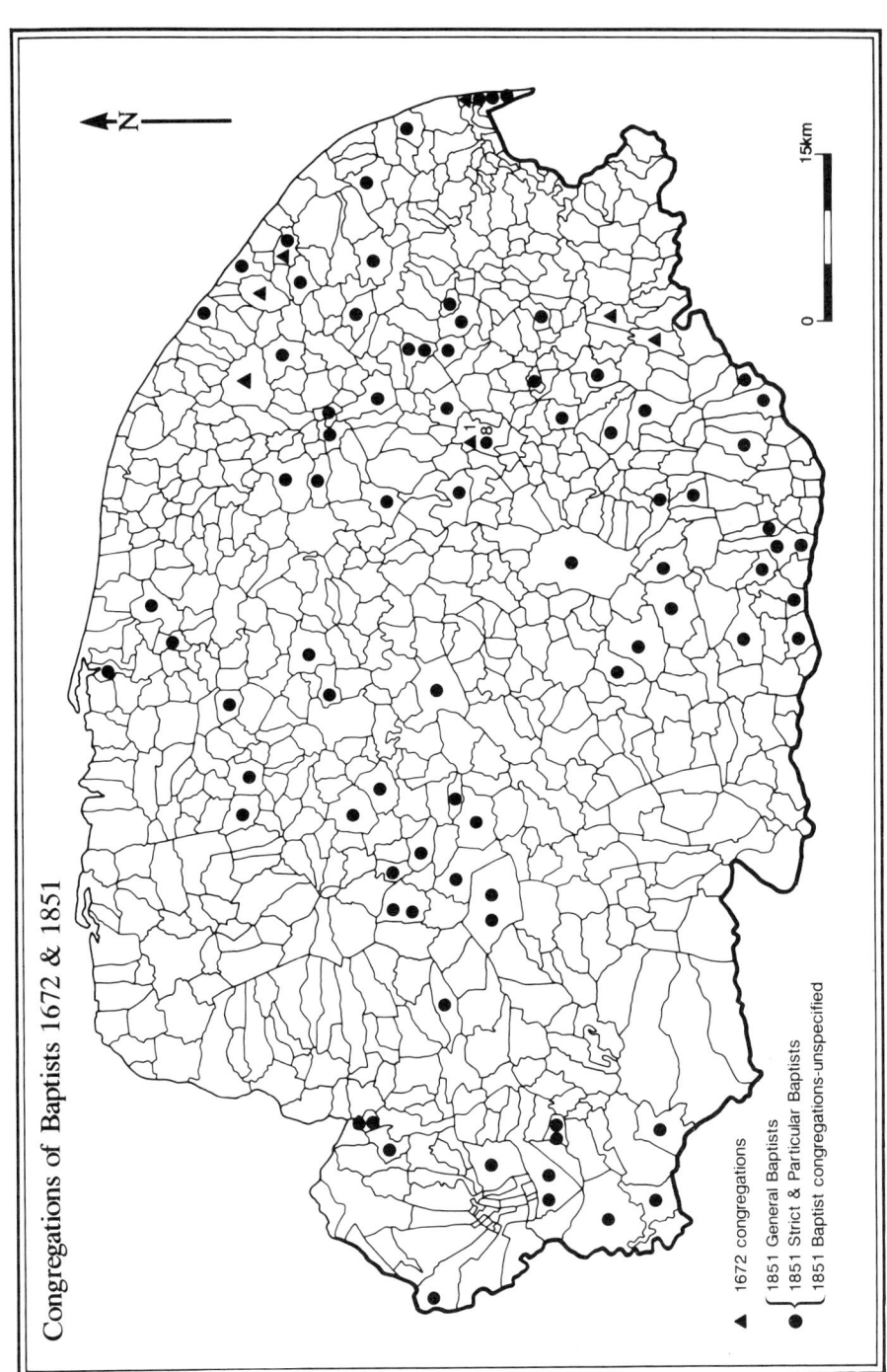

MAPPING NONCONFORMITY IN NORFOLK

JANET EDE and NORMA VIRGOE

The publication of the *Historical Atlas of Suffolk* in 1988[1] was greeted with such enthusiasm that it was decided to produce a similar volume for Norfolk. Amongst the many maps illustrating the county's history, one showing Protestant nonconformity has been included in order to parallel that of the Suffolk atlas and identical symbols have been used in order to facilitate comparison.[2]

In order to be able to compare the Norfolk and Suffolk maps meaningfully, it was decided to use the same original sources which not only provided similar types of information, but also fixed the same points of time at which particular congregations existed. The nature of the sources used means that the map records the existence of congregations not their buildings. The year 1672 was taken as the earlier date at which congregations were recorded on the map; the Declaration of Indulgence of that year allowed freedom of worship provided that the premises used were registered and licences obtained. The existence of congregations was noted as a result of the Declaration and their premises named and, though these were usually domestic buildings, warehouses, storerooms, industrial premises or barns, rather than purpose-built chapels or meeting-houses, yet the specific meeting was licensed and recorded. Absent from this register are the meetings of the Society of Friends so the list of their gatherings made in 1667 has been used to supplement the information provided by the 1672 registrations.[3] The

---

[1] *An Historical Atlas of Suffolk*, ed. David Dymond and Edward Martin, Suffolk County Council and Suffolk Institute of Archaeology and History, 1988

[2] The maps illustrating this article were drawn by Phillip Judge

[3] List of meeting places of the Society of Friends supplied by the Librarian, Friends' House, London, 1955, Norfolk and Norwich Library Service, Local History Department, C289.6

Religious Census of 1851 provided the later date for recording the congregations on the distribution map.[4] This article provides an opportunity to present the information shown in the Atlas in more detailed form.

Apart from the large towns of Yarmouth and King's Lynn and the City of Norwich, Old Dissent in the later seventeenth century was clustered in two main areas of Norfolk. There was a notable concentration of congregations in the north-east of the county and a spread along the Waveney Valley in the south. This latter group relates to the spread of Dissenting congregations in the adjacent areas of north and north-east Suffolk in this earlier period. It may be that the geographical character of these two areas of Norfolk explain their support of Old Dissent. In both regions there was an absence of large estates and overweening landowners; farms were relatively small and farmers modestly well off - such people were well-known for their independence of mind and support for Dissent.

In 1672, early Baptist congregations were entirely confined to the two main Dissenting areas in the north-east and the south of the county. By 1851

---

[4] Religious Census, 1851; *British Sessional Papers*, House of Commons, 1852/3, vol. lxxxix. The census summary gives the following comparative figures:

	Norfolk	Suffolk
Independent	49	90
Baptist - General	3	-
General New Connexion	6	-
Particular	67	78
Not otherwise defined	15	13
Society of Friends	15	6
Unitarian	7	3
Wesleyan Methodist Original Connexion	213	84
New Connexion	1	-
Primitive Methodist	254	72
Bible Christians	2	-
Wesleyan Methodist Association	2	2
Wesleyan Reformers	44	3
Lady Huntingdon's Connexion	2	-
Sandemanians	1	-
New Church	1	-
Brethren	-	3
Isolated Congregations	19	10
Latter Day Saints	13	3

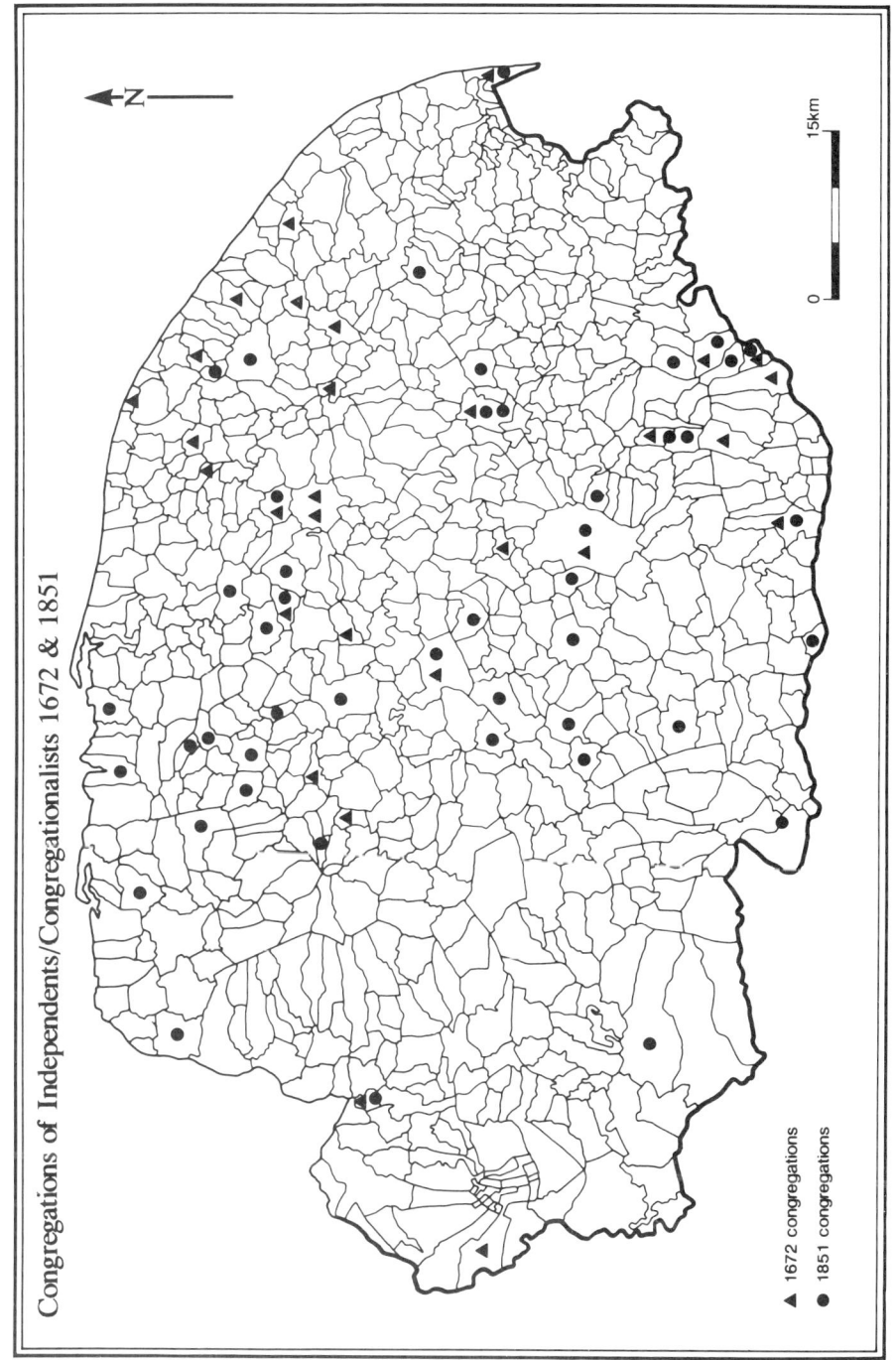

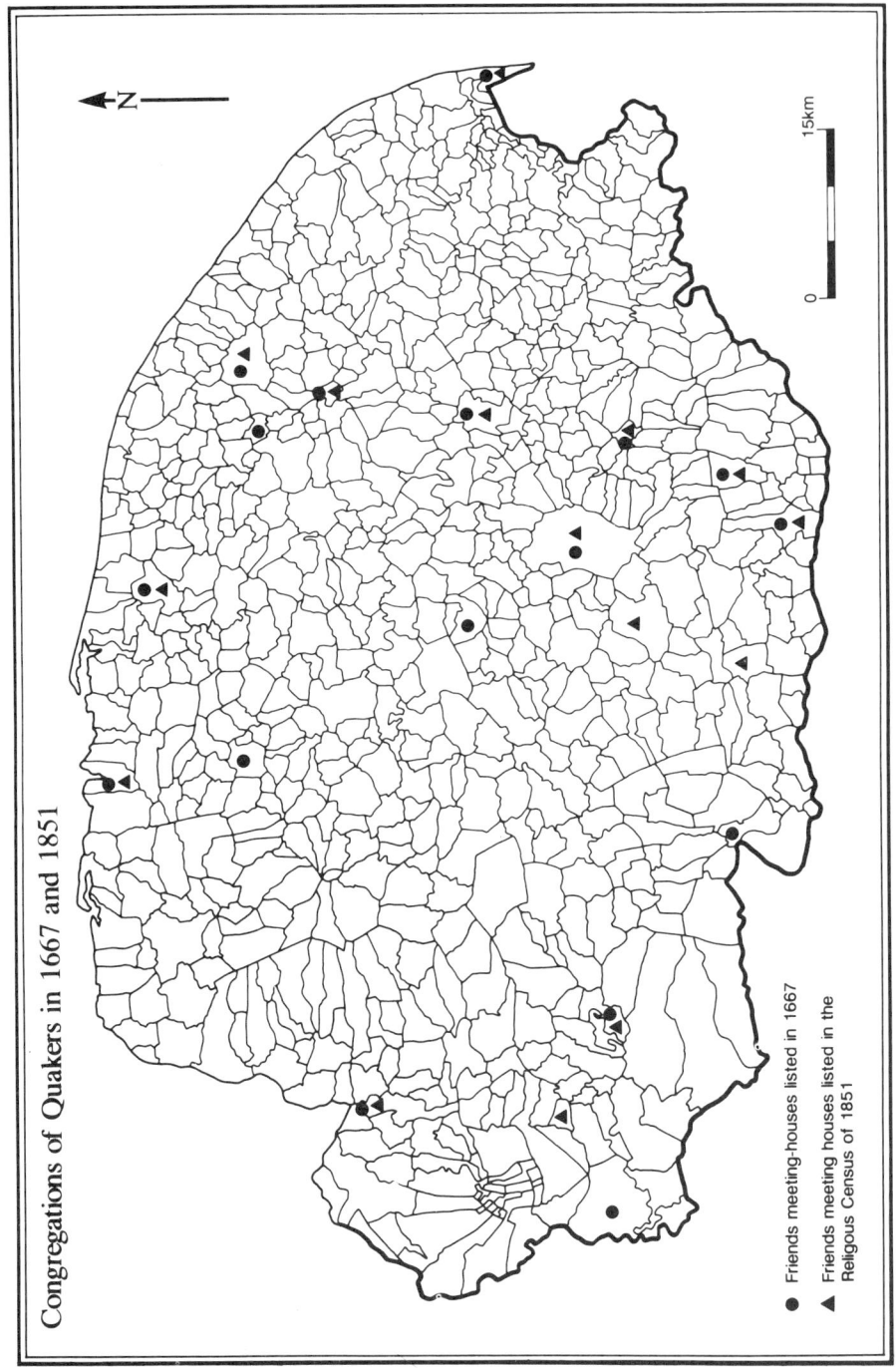

almost all of these early congregations had disappeared and had been supplanted by a substantial sprinkling in the east of the county and in a diagonal band from the north coast around Blakeney through the middle of the county to the Cambridgeshire border. However, Norfolk in 1851 had fewer Baptists than any of the surrounding counties.[5]

Greater continuity is demonstrated amongst the Independent and Congregational groups. The earlier congregations again clustered in the north-east and south; by 1851 the north-eastern concentration had moved to the centre-north of the county whilst in the south new congregations had multiplied and new groups were clustered round the centres of old meetings. Once again there were fewer congregations in Norfolk than in nearby counties; the comparable figures for Norfolk were forty-nine and for Suffolk ninety-three. Chapel records such as those at Guestwick show that people were prepared to travel considerable distances for worship.

There was little change in the total numbers of meetings of the Society of Friends from the 1667 list of Quaker meetings when seventeen are recorded to the Census of 1851 when there were fifteen; continuity existed in the case of twelve meetings. However, one of the weaknesses in recording at fixed points of time is that meetings may be established, flourish, decline and die without any record of their existence appearing on the map, and with Quaker meetings those of Hingham and Swaffham fall into this category. The map confirms that membership of the Society of Friends had reached a low ebb by the middle of the nineteenth century as a consequence of the stress on spiritual individualism and passivity, the excessive use of silence, and a disparagement of the ministry of the spoken word.

Presbyterians in the late seventeenth century were typically found in the north-east and south of the county with an isolated congregation at King's Lynn. The great doctrinal dispute in the early eighteenth century dealt a severe blow to Presbyterianism and many congregations changed their theological standpoint, a considerable number of them embracing Unitarianism. All the Presbyterian congregations in Norfolk had died out by 1851. Seven Unitarian congregations were in existence by this time, but only Diss, King's Lynn and Norwich had both a 1672 Presbyterian congregation and a later Unitarian one.

By 1851 the Church of Latter Day Saints had become a significant factor

---

[5] John D. Gay, *The Geography of Religion in England*, 1971, map 27

in English religious life. Its membership declined dramatically after this date and the mid-nineteenth century peak of congregations was not again equalled until the 1960s. The group had begun in the United States of America in 1822 and missionaries first visited Britain in 1837, seeking converts and encouraging emigration to join the American community. In 1851 there were thirteen congregations in Norfolk whilst in Suffolk there were only three.

Interestingly there were no congregations of Plymouth Brethren in the county in 1851. One Sandemanian group, one Swedenborgian, one Calvinist, two Countess of Huntingdon's Connexion chapels and fifteen non-denominational congregations are recorded by the Census of 1851. These were almost all in the largest towns.

Without doubt, the most striking feature of the nonconformist distribution maps is the enormous dominance of Methodism throughout the county. The only areas without Methodist chapels are a few of the Breckland parishes and those in heathland areas immediately inland from the north Norfolk coast, both very thinly populated regions; there is also a small circular area almost empty of congregations immediately to the east of Norwich where parishes also had low populations.

The density of Methodist chapels in Norfolk is far greater than in any of the surrounding counties apart from Lincolnshire. This appears to bear out the contention that where Old Dissent was strong, Methodism had less success: Norfolk, a county where Old Dissent was circumscribed, was wide open to Methodism. In addition, poor rural conditions, particularly the large numbers of landless labourers, together with the discontent generated by the commutation of tithes, encouraged hostility towards the large landowners and the clergy and bolstered the great explosion of Methodism in Norfolk.

Primitive Methodism, which reached the county in 1820, appealed particularly to farm labourers and in its local preachers threw up leaders who worked to improve the conditions of agricultural workers. Norfolk, together with the East Riding of Yorkshire, was the strongest centre of Primitive Methodism in England with no less than 234 chapels in 1851.

In many parishes more than one congregation of Methodists existed and in some larger parishes several Methodist chapels were built, the record being held by Upwell which had three Wesleyan chapels, four Primitive Methodist and three Wesleyan Reform as well as a Baptist chapel.

In 1849 a sudden expansion of Methodist places of worship occurred when a formal split took place amongst the Wesleyans. The break-away group known as the Wesleyan Reformers or frequently in Norfolk as

MAPPING NONCONFORMITY IN NORFOLK

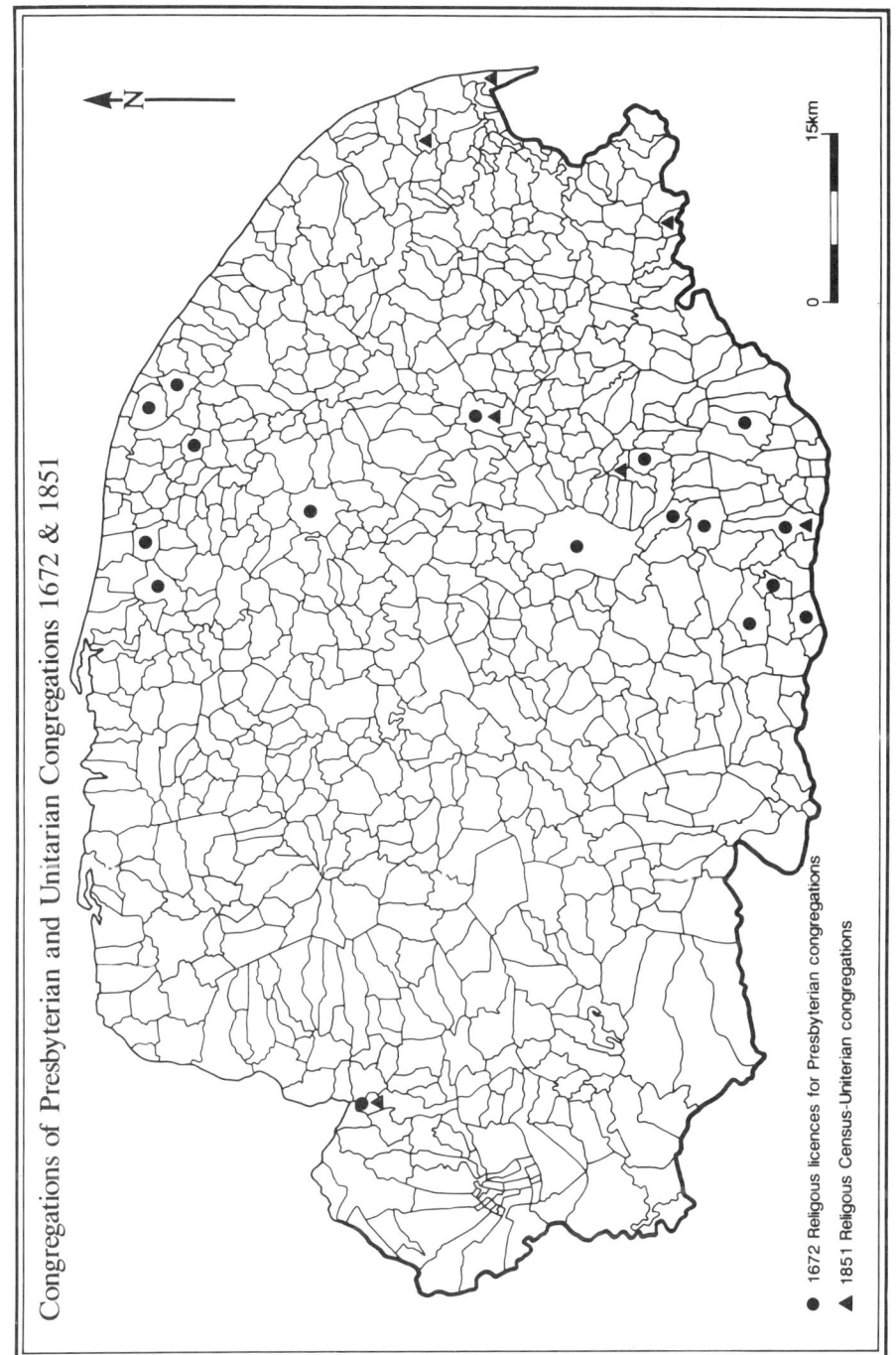

MAPPING NONCONFORMITY IN NORFOLK

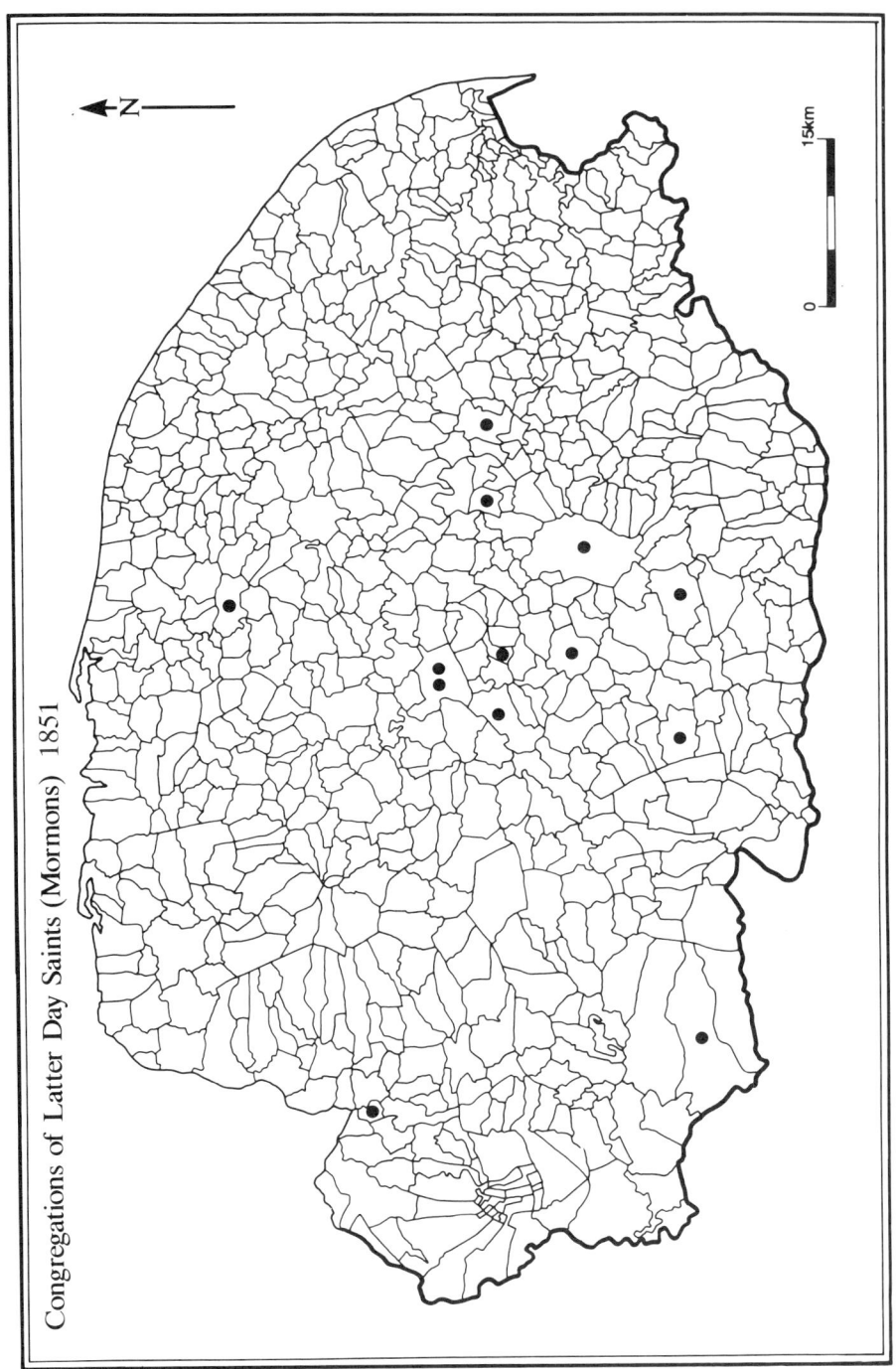

MAPPING NONCONFORMITY IN NORFOLK

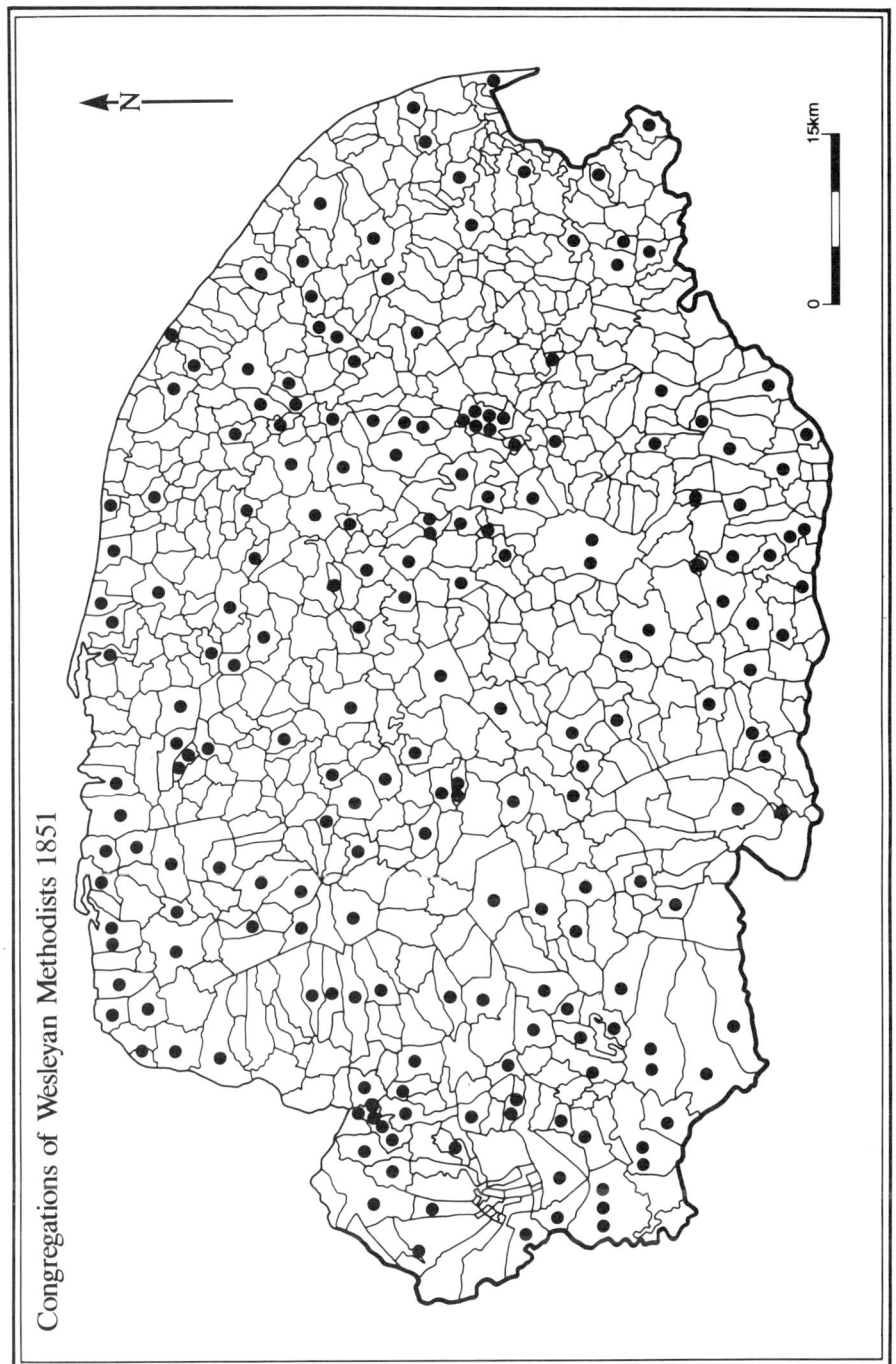

MAPPING NONCONFORMITY IN NORFOLK

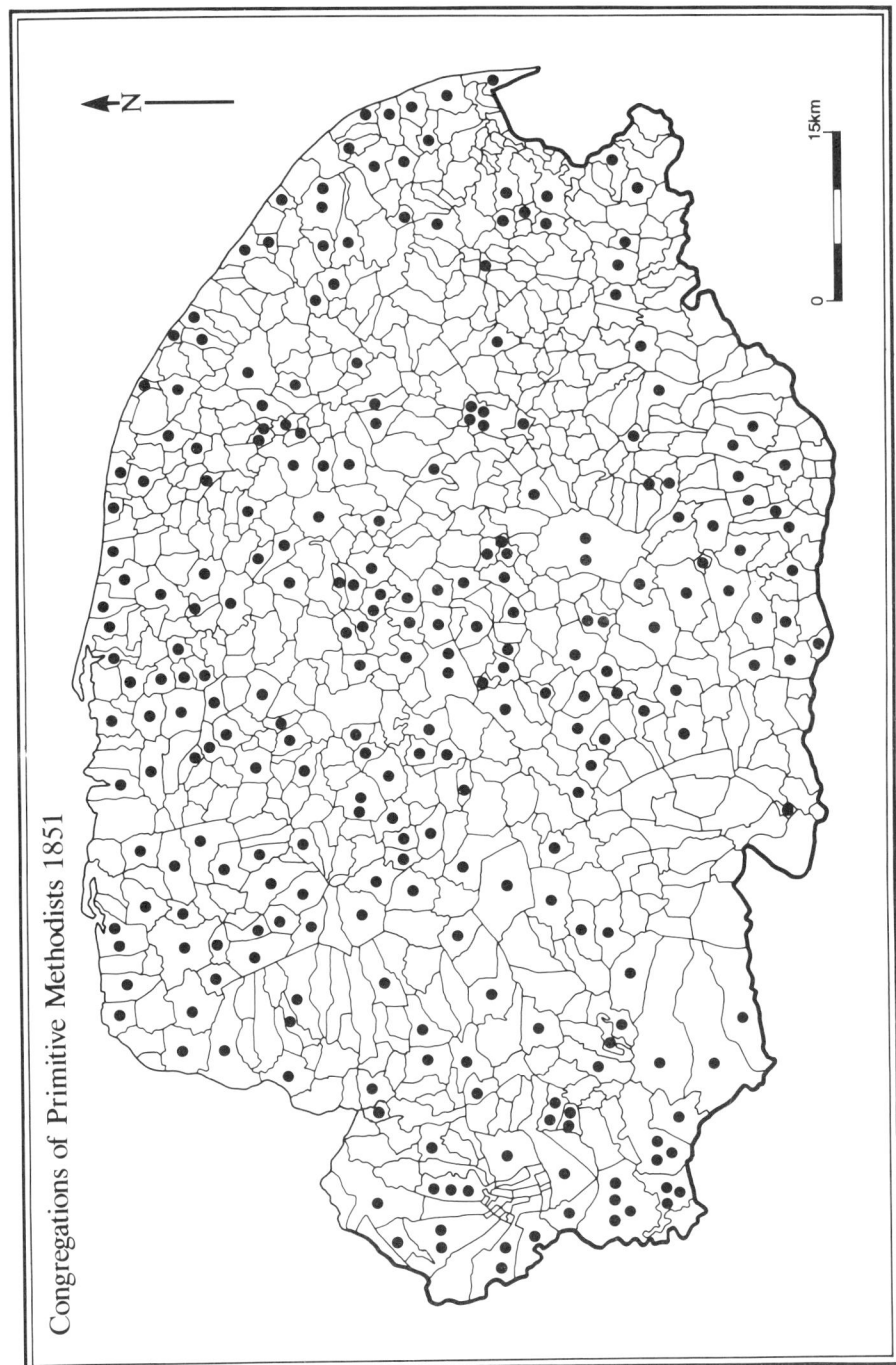

Congregations of Primitive Methodists 1851

MAPPING NONCONFORMITY IN NORFOLK

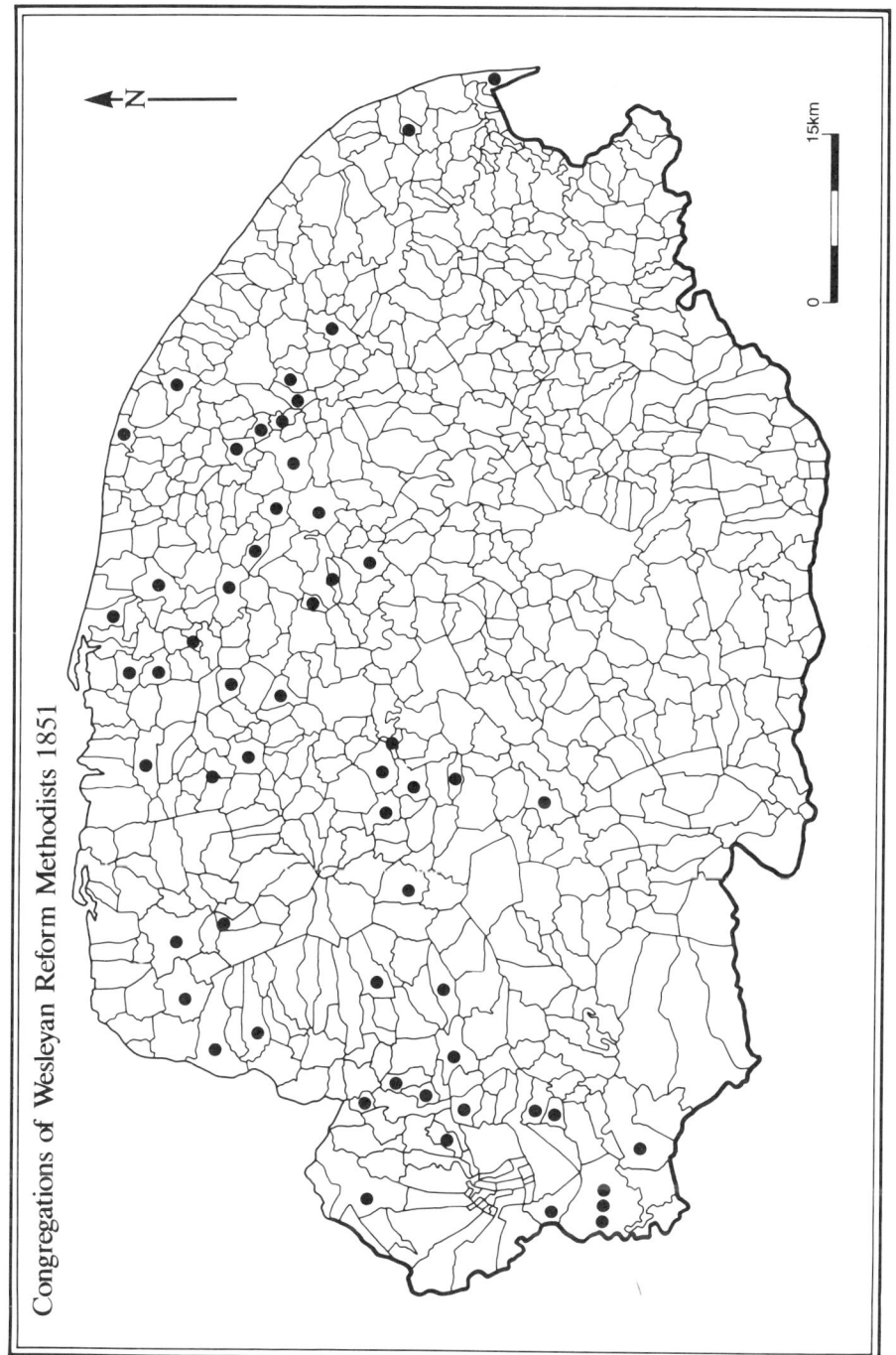

Wesleyan Branch was particularly strong in the north and west of the county. Sometimes whole chapels transferred allegiance; sometimes a new chapel was founded by whichever group was in the minority; in other instances the Reformers met in temporary accommodation just as all the other Dissenting denominations had done at their outset. The Census picked up the bitterness accompanying the split. At Lenwade the Wesleyans reported that 'violent and disgraceful proceedings nearly destroyed the congregation' and the resultant group of dissident Reformers noted that they met in a public room at the King's Head. 'There would be a larger congregation if the place was more suitable as there is a great objection made by some of the reformers to its being a public house ...'. Norfolk was a county where the Wesleyan Reform movement was particularly strong with forty-four recorded congregations in 1851; not one was recorded for Suffolk.[6]

By 1851, therefore, the county was thickly populated with nonconformist congregations. Methodism was attracting enormous support whilst the older forms of Dissent shared in the revival of spiritual interest initiated by the Wesleys in the second half of the eighteenth century and continued by their followers.

[6] Although the map of Protestant nonconformity in the *Historical Atlas of Suffolk* was compiled from the 1851 Religious Census returns and shows no Wesleyan Reform congregations, yet the summary of Census figures in *British Sessional Papers* states that there were three congregations of Wesleyan Reformers in Suffolk. This is not the only discrepancy between the Census returns and the summary.

THE NORFOLK NONCONFORMIST CHAPELS SURVEY: SOME PRELIMINARY RESULTS

TOM WILLIAMSON

Introduction

Since 1987, the Norfolk Archaeological Rescue Group, in association with the Centre of East Anglian studies, has been carrying out a comprehensive study of nonconformist chapels and meeting-houses in Norfolk. This research was begun in response to the rapid disappearance of the county's rich legacy of nonconformist architecture. But it was also motivated by a more general desire to understand the relationship between architecture and belief, and to place both within a wider social and economic context.

Our approach has, therefore, been that of the archaeologist rather than the art historian. We are primarily interested in these buildings, not as 'works of art' (although many no doubt are that), but as evidence for religious, economic and social history. And *evidence* is the right word. These buildings are not merely *reflections* of activity, manifestations of beliefs and activities which we can learn all about from documents and texts. They constitute, we would argue, a body of historical evidence in their own right. And it is because of this, rather than for reasons of mere antiquarian interest, that they need to be recorded before being destroyed or drastically converted to other uses. This particular approach means that we are interested in *all* nonconformist and Dissenting structures regardless of their antiquity or supposed artistic merit.

Methodology

There are well over 700 surviving chapels and meeting-houses in Norfolk, a number so great that it was realised, at any early stage, that a comprehensive survey of each building - complete with measured plans, elevations etc - was beyond the resources of the group. Instead, we adopted a programme of surveying the buildings at two quite distinct levels. The first level of survey, which is now nearing completion, was undertaken by a large and able group of volunteers who recorded basic information about the age, size, style, location, fittings and structural history of all the chapels in the county. This was carried out using standardised record forms and it is these which form the primary archive of the survey. This information is also, however, being transferred on to a computer database which allows us to analyse the mass of data collected with speed and efficiency, and thus to identify broad groups of buildings which are characteristic of particular periods and/or denominations. The second level of survey, which has not yet begun, will take the form of a more detailed examination of a sample of these characteristic groups, taking a small number of buildings, representative of each, and recording them in detail.

The first level survey is itself only partially completed and the brief discussion that follows should be treated as only very provisional. It is based on an analysis of over 300 rural chapels in the county for which the recorded information - including, crucially, the date of initial construction - is reliable and complete.

The Chronology of Building Activity

> Awakened from their eighteenth-century slumbers by the trumpet-call of the Methodist revival, Congregational and Baptist preachers radiated outwards from their traditional Puritan strongholds, plunging ever more deeply into hitherto un-evangelised fields.[1]

Figure 1, which shows the number of new chapels and meeting-houses begun in Norfolk in each decade after 1770, suggests that the county shared in the upsurge of enthusiasm and energy described by Sellars. The graph reveals a steady increase in the number of new foundations up until the 1860s, the 'golden decade' of nonconformity. The details of the graph also mirror features noted elsewhere in the country. Thus, for example, a peak of

---

[1] Ian Sellars, *Nineteenth-Century Nonconformity*. 1977, p.1

THE NORFOLK NONCONFORMIST CHAPELS SURVEY

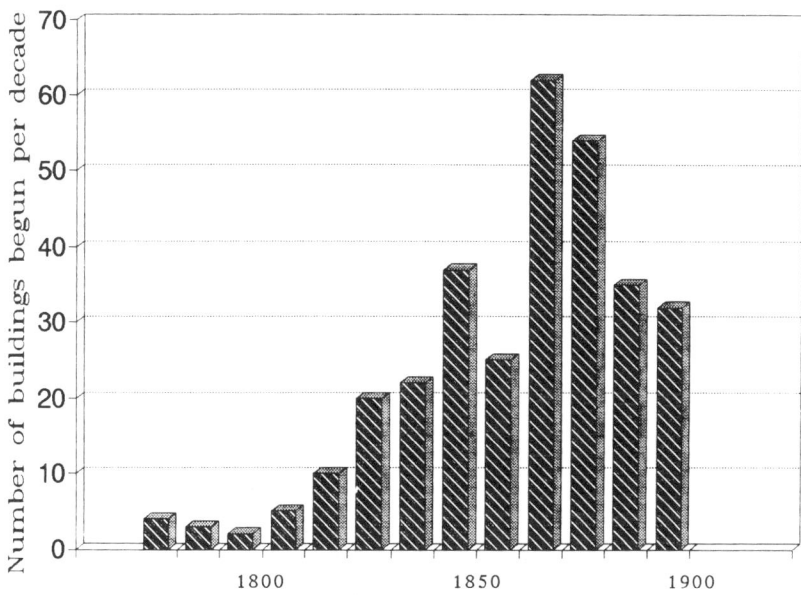

Figure 1: Numbers of chapels constructed: all denominations

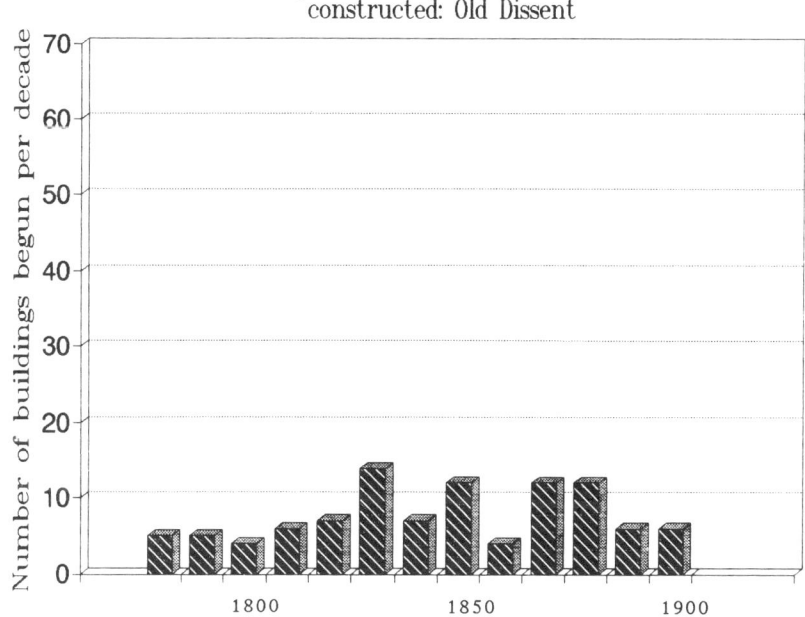

Figure 2: Numbers of chapels constructed: Old Dissent

THE NORFOLK NONCONFORMIST CHAPELS SURVEY

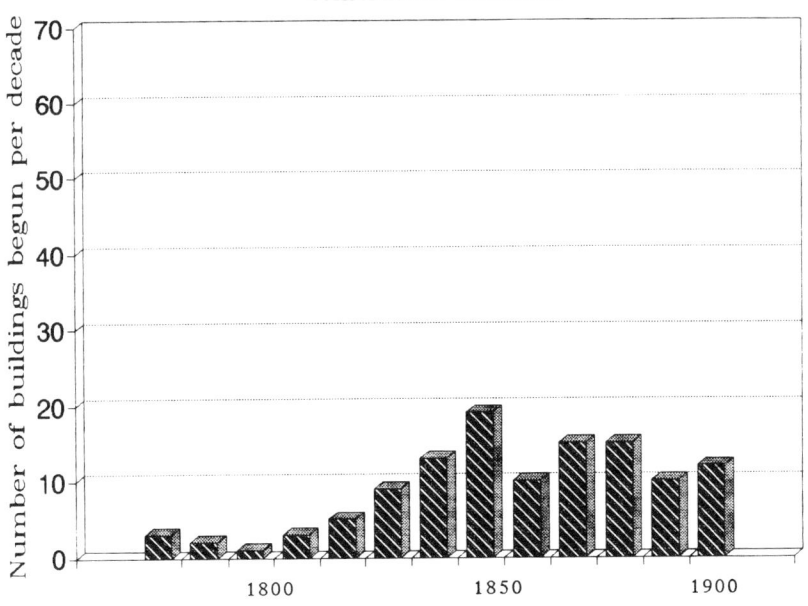

Figure 3: Numbers of chapels constructed: Methodist

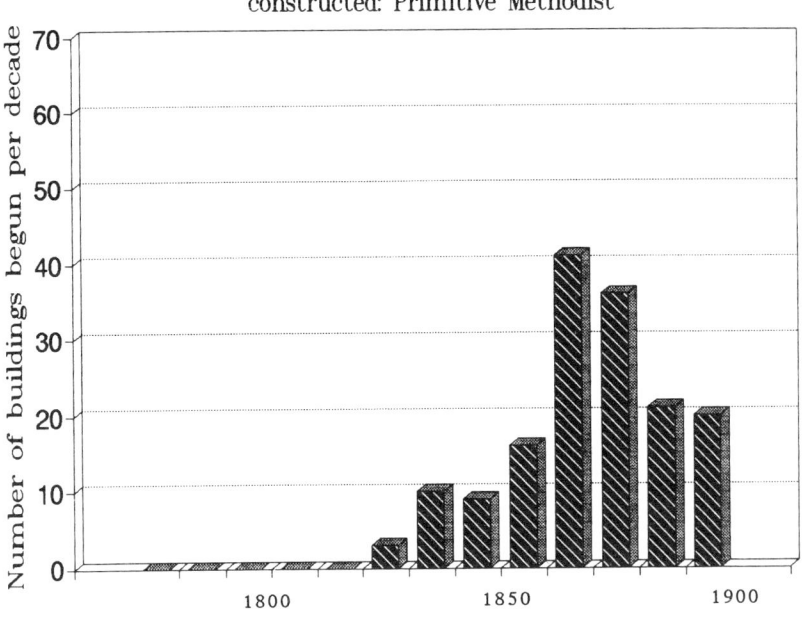

Figure 4: Numbers of chapels constructed: Primitive Methodist

building activity in the 1840s was followed by a slight trough:

> Strangely however there followed a ten-year hiatus before advance was resumed again, and the 1850s were fruitless years for most denominations.[2]

Yet in a number of ways this graph is misleading. In lumping together the building activities of a number of quite different religious groups, it gives the false impression that the fortunes of all were much the same. It is, therefore, more interesting and informative to separate out the building activities of three broad (and slightly arbitrary) groupings: the Primitive Methodists, other kinds of Methodists, and the various forms of Old Dissent.

Figure 2 shows that new foundations by Baptists, Independents/Congregationalists, Friends and Unitarians continued at a fairly steady, although fairly low, level throughout the late eighteenth and nineteenth centuries with only a slight trough in the 1860s, and slight peaks in the 1820s and 40s. The Methodists, in contrast, display a very different pattern, with (as we might expect) a clear increase in the number of new foundations, decade by decade, through the early part of the nineteenth century, rising to a peak in the 1850s (figure 3). This was followed by a slight decline, although for the most part the number of new foundations continued at a steady rate until the end of the century. But it is the Primitive Methodists who display the most dramatic pattern (figure 4). The numbers of their new foundations increased steadily through to the 1850s, and then dramatically in the following decade. They then declined slowly to the end of the century, although even in the 1890s an average of around two new Primitive Methodist chapels were still begun each year. The upsurge in the Primitives' building activities in the 1860s is remarkable and largely accounts for the *overall* increase in the numbers of nonconformist chapels in this decade. In Norfolk, at least, the 'Golden Decade' largely belonged to the Primitives.

Graphs are reassuring, but often misleading, things and it is important to stress what these particular examples do *not* show. They are not graphs of belief: they will not closely reflect the number or the size of congregations. As Dolby observed long ago, the great majority of congregations began 'in a humble and homely way', meeting for fellowship in private houses. Only as numbers increased, and sufficient support became available, were plans

---

[2] *Ibid*, p.9

made for erecting a preaching-house or chapel.[3]

This was, moreover, a recurrent pattern displayed by most emerging denominations. Arthur Patterson described how in Great Yarmouth in 1823 the Primitive Methodists began meeting in

> The old Hayloft ... an upper story of a stable that had done duty also as a carpenter's shop. The length of the building was some twenty feet, or thereabouts ... Old-fashioned pantiles covered the roof; and the building, furnished with stiffly built seats, backed and painted, afforded moderate - only moderate - accommodation for some fifty or sixty worshippers. Such was the first real 'home' of our stalwart parents.[4]

The rate at which, in any area, different groups crossed the threshold from such makeshift accommodation to purpose-built edifices must have depended on a range of factors beyond the size of their congregations or the strength of their convictions. Above all, it must have been related to the wealth of the social groups from which each denomination drew its support and also - at least to some extent - to the general economic climate. Thus, all the graphs so far discussed are problematic: the chronology of the building activities they display must have been the outcome of the interplay of a number of factors. They raise questions rather than supply ready-made answers. To what extent, for example, does the phenomenal post-1850s increase in Primitive Methodist building activity reflect not just an increase in the number of believers, but the increasing numbers of individuals from the more affluent sections of rural society being attracted to the congregations, people able to donate the money and land necessary for chapel construction? In a similar way, we might ask how far the dip in the building activities of most congregations in the 1850s reflects the economic fortunes of the social groups who provided the money and land for chapel construction rather than any faltering in their enthusiasm.

---

[3] G.W. Dolby, *The Architectural Expression of Methodism*, 1964, p.23

[4] A.H. Patterson, *From Hayloft to Temple: Primitive Methodism in Yarmouth*, Norwich, 1903, p.12

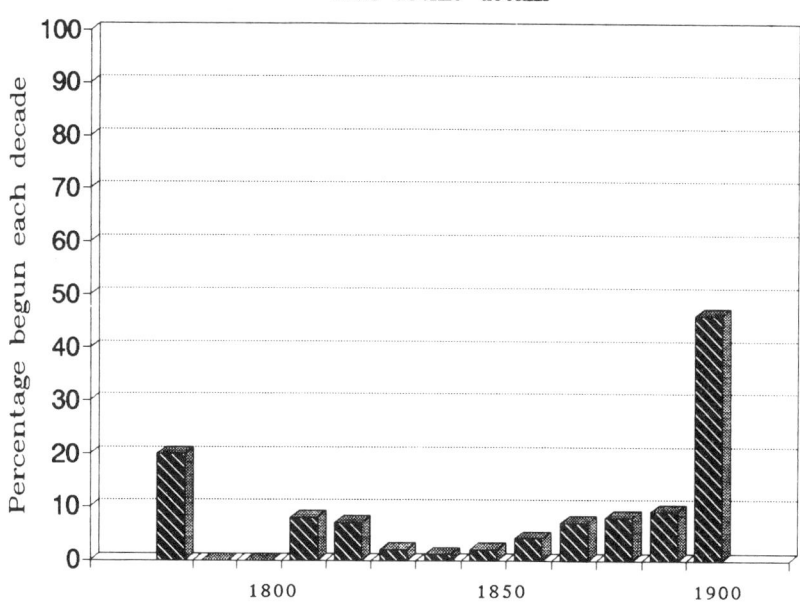

Figure 5: Percentage of chapels with 'Gothic' details

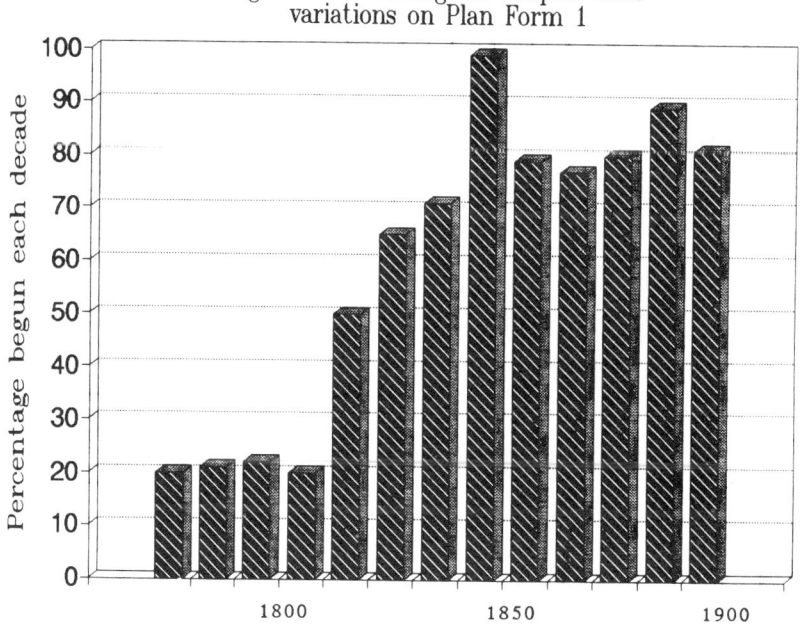

Figure 6: Percentage of chapels with variations on Plan Form 1

THE NORFOLK NONCONFORMIST CHAPELS SURVEY

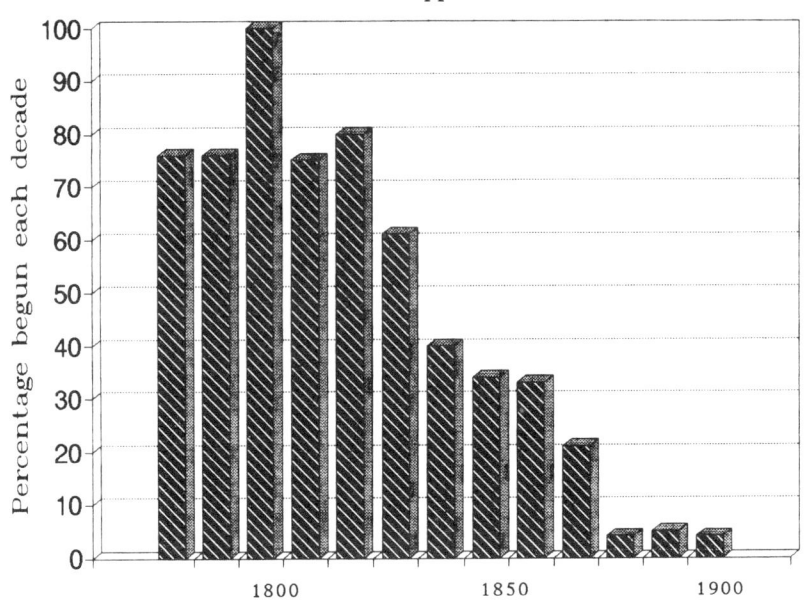

Figure 7: Percentage of chapels with hipped roofs

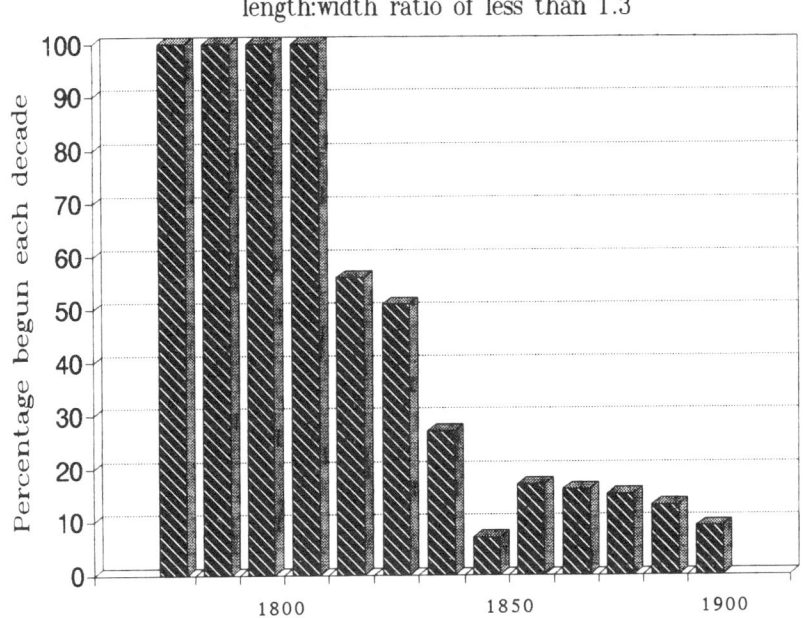

Figure 8: Percentage of chapels with length:width ratio of less than 1.3

THE NORFOLK NONCONFORMIST CHAPELS SURVEY

The Development of Chapel Architecture

The data collected so far, valuable though it is, tells us only part of the story and much more work on the documentary material is necessary to see chapel-building in its social and economic, as well as religious, context. But, as I have already emphasised, the buildings are also useful as primary data: they are not merely illustrations of what we can learn from written sources.

In some cases, the survey results provide only a slight modification of received wisdom. The adoption of 'gothic' styles of architecture for chapels in the county is an interesting example of this. In 1850, F.J. Jobson averred that:

> our Reformation forefathers, whose principles we hold, evinced a disposition to desert Gothic Architecture, and leave it to the Romish church. They ... erected 'Meeting-houses', as irregular and as plain, in design and character, as the stables they built for horses, or the barns they raised for corn ... But now that time has been given for calm reflection, and opportunity for avoiding extremes, Truth in Architecture is appearing; and the modern successors of the Puritans work not a little Gothic into their houses of worship ...[5]

The evidence from Norfolk, however, indicates a slightly different pattern. Binfield's 'nonconformity of soaring spires' was not greeted with enthusiasm in rural Norfolk: the gothic revival was very slow to take root and only in the decades after 1900 were more than 12% of chapels constructed in what might even loosely be termed a gothic style. Figure 5 will please those who, with Martin Briggs, see gothic as a short-lived and lamentable abberation from the true principles of Puritan architecture.[6]

But the graph is interesting for another reason: it *appears* to show that gothic was being adopted as a style for chapels much earlier than a reading of Jobson and his contemporaries might suggest. To some extent, this is an illusion caused by problems of definition and by the need to simplify a complex reality when recording a large data-set using standardised record forms. The late eighteenth-century buildings deemed 'gothic' by the survey team were so classified simply because their windows and/or doors are of

---

[5] F.J. Jobson, *Chapel and School Architecture*, 1880, pp.39-40

[6] M.S. Briggs, *Protestant Architecture and its Future*, 1945

pointed form. Such buildings are hardly gothic structures in the sense in which Jobson would have used the term, but their appearance has some significance: they are, for the most part, large rather urbane meeting-houses, showing the influence of gentleman's Regency gothic. The adoption of such gothic details may suggest that the broadly vernacular or classical inspiration of most eighteenth-century chapels owed more to general fashions in architecture than it did to any conscious rejection of an architectural style associated with the established church.

The pattern of acceptance of gothic architecture shown by figure 8 appears, on present evidence, to be shared by all denominations. Indeed, it we ignore certain comparatively minor details of the layout of interiors, there appears to have been little difference between contemporary chapels being erected by different denominations. By and large, differences in the style and layout of chapels are related to chronology not to belief.

This is particularly clear with regard to the plans of the buildings. In the eighteenth century, there were a variety of plan forms, many involving two doors, and/or with entry along the long sides of the building. After 1800, however, all denominations experienced the rise of plan forms falling within our category 1; i.e. buildings with a single door in the *short* side, facing a pulpit or other areas of ceremonial significance located near or against the other short side (figure 6). The rise to dominance of this plan form - which after 1840 always accounted for between 75% and 100% of nonconformist buildings - was closely related to other changes. In particular, there was a marked decline, in the early decades of the nineteenth century, in the number of buildings constructed with hipped or half-hipped, as opposed to gable, roofs (figure 7). And this, in turn, was related to changes in the dimensions of the buildings, the ratio of their width to their length. For obvious structural reasons, the more closely the plan of a building corresponds to a square, the more likely it is that the structure will have a hipped rather than a gabled roof. And it is not surprising, therefore, to find that the same period saw a dramatic reduction in the numbers of buildings being constructed with square, or near-square, plans (including those constructed with their sides in the ratio of 21:18 favoured by Wesley). Figure 8 shows this development clearly. Buildings with a length:width ratio of less than 1.3 declined suddenly and dramatically in the decades after 1800: before this, they had been almost universal. This, we believe, should not simply be interpreted as a change in architectural 'fashion', but as an expression of changes in the nature of nonconformity itself.

Sellars has drawn attention to changes in the nature of nonconformist worship in the late eighteenth and nineteenth centuries and its relationship with the overall increase in the numbers of nonconformists.

> The type of preaching which underlay this achievement was fervent exhortation rather than intellectual argument[7]

– a development which was not universally favoured by older traditionalists, 'for whom theological disputation was meat and drink'.[8] Chapels were increasingly a stage for a drama rather than an arena for intellectual enquiry. And so, in the buildings erected by most nonconformists, we see a marked shift in architectural form: a change which, to judge from the Norfolk evidence, went hand in hand with the overall increase in the numbers of congregations.

Location and Setting

This pattern of shared development extends not just to the architecture of the chapels, but also to their location and setting. The Toleration Acts had given grudging toleration to Dissenting groups. But, until late in the eighteenth century, even this was considered excessive in some quarters. Not only mobs, but members of the government establishment, were slow to accept Dissent: as late as 1800, the Pitt administration considered the repeal of the Toleration Acts. But things changed rapidly thereafter, with the passing of the so-called 'Little Toleration Act' in 1811; with the repeal of the Test and Corporation Acts in 1829; and with the passing of the Burial Acts of 1847, 1857 and 1880.

The insecurity felt by congregations in the eighteenth century is, it is sometimes suggested, reflected in the often isolated or hidden locations of early chapels and meeting-houses. Conversely, increasing toleration and the decline of mob activity was reflected in the construction of chapels in more visible, public positions. To some extent, the Norfolk evidence bears out this general observation: figure 9 shows the percentage of chapels considered to

---

[7] Sellars, *op.cit*, p.2

[8] *Ibid*, p.3

be in isolated locations or constructed down an alley or loke, as subjectively assessed by members of the recording team. Buildings in such locations declined as an overall proportion of the total number constructed as the nineteenth century progressed: those fronting on a main street, in contrast, became more common.

Yet preliminary analysis also suggests that the relationship between location and public attitudes to nonconformity needs more careful examination. For it is not entirely clear how the positioning of an urban chapel down a back alley rather than on a main street or in a market place would necessarily have made it less of a target for the mob. It is not as if the inhabitants of a small market town would have been unaware of the building's existence. The hidden or peripheral locations of many early chapels may have a more complex explanation. On the one hand, it might in part reflect economic factors - the relative low cost of marginal land or of inconvenient backyard plots. An increase in the number of buildings being constructed in more central and prominent positions might, therefore, be related to the changing economic fortunes of the Dissenting groups. On the other hand, this development may reflect changes in the more general psychological attitude of the congregations. The earlier locational pattern may represent a turning away from the hustle and bustle of the village nucleus and the market place: a shift to more public and prominent locations, in turn, might indicate a greater feeling of ease, confidence and - above all - integration with the wide community.

This development in the location of chapels ran parallel with another important change. Early meeting-houses had, almost always, their own burial grounds, usually adjacent to or surrounding the building. Where - as in the case of the Aylsham Baptists - the building originally lacked a burial ground, it usually gained one at a slightly later date. But in the decades after 1800, the number of new buildings with burial grounds began to decline and by 1850 very few new foundations had their own burial plot (figure 10). Their congregations were evidently being buried elsewhere, principally no doubt in the new urban cemeteries which, following the opening of the Rosary in Norwich, in 1821, proliferated in the smaller towns. A building set within a burial ground is more obviously a separate *community* than one otherwise located. In the former case, the living and the dead share a single plot, representing both distinctiveness and continuity: and most especially, when

THE NORFOLK NONCONFORMIST CHAPELS SURVEY

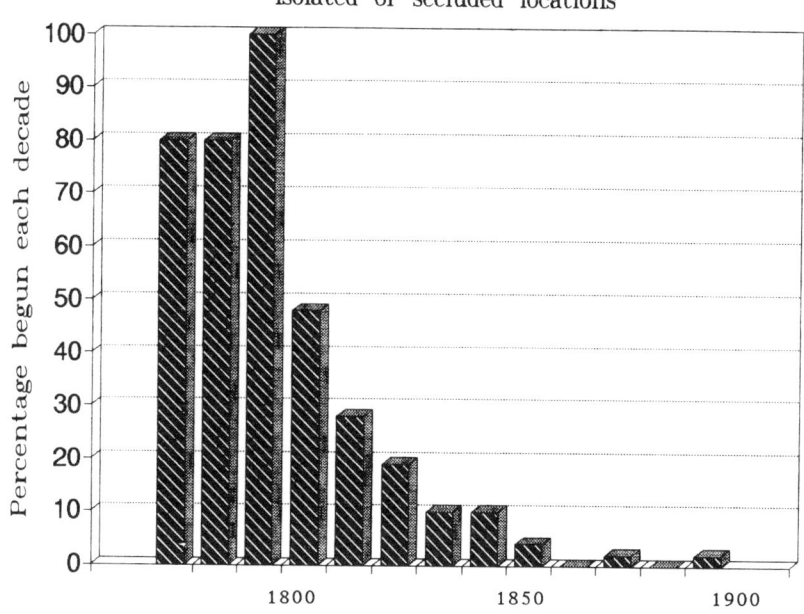

Figure 9: Percentage of chapels in 'isolated' or 'secluded' locations

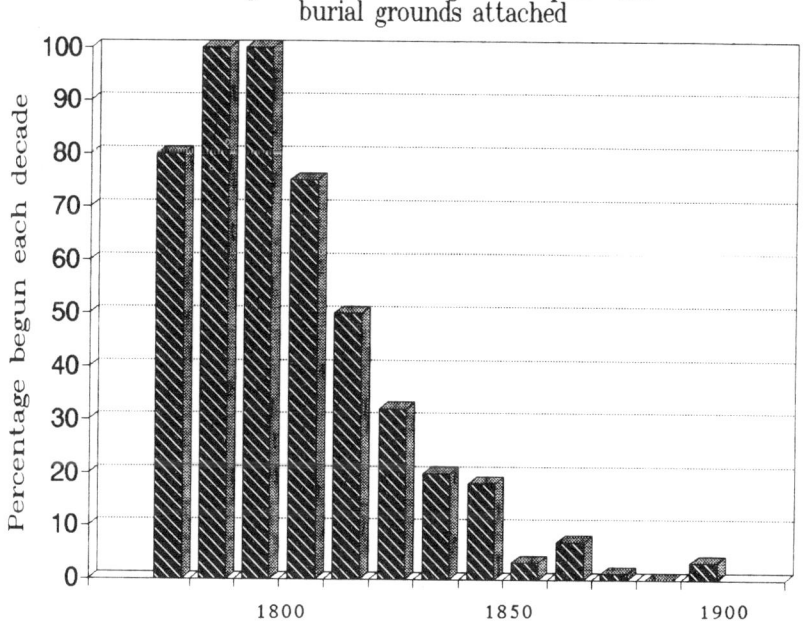

Figure 10: Percentage of chapels with burial grounds attached

the building is located in a marginal or hidden location. The decline in the importance of the chapel burial ground may once again represent the increasing integration of nonconformists within the wider community.

Conclusion

Taken together, these results suggest that meeting-houses and chapels in rural Norfolk followed a clear pattern of development, a pattern largely shared by all denominations. Crucial changes occurred in the decades after 1800. Up to this point, there had been few purpose-built nonconformist chapels of any kind in the county. Those that did exist were mainly of approximately square plan, although some were rectangular with doors positioned in the long sides, and they displayed a variety of internal arrangements. They were often, although by no means always, constructed in comparatively marginal or hidden locations; and they usually had burial grounds attached. Such a pattern accords well with Sellar's description of their users and patrons as 'a fellowship of believers united against the world'.[9]

From the 1810s, however, things changed rapidly. There was an explosion in numbers and a move to a standardised plan form, one perhaps suited to more dramatic forms of religious experience. These buildings were increasingly built without burial grounds and in more prominent and public positions. A change in the meaning of the buildings and in the role of their congregations appears to be indicated: a shift from Dissent to nonconformity; from meeting-house to chapel.

[9] *Ibid*, p.78

POLITICS OR QUIETISM:
THE SOCIAL HISTORY OF NONCONFORMITY

ALUN HOWKINS

In an address given to the leaders' meeting of Eastbourne Pevensey Road Wesleyan chapel in January 1912, the minister, the Reverend H.C. Morton

> emphasized the fact that he considered the church was becoming deluged with a flood of amusements, social gatherings and Musical evenings and pleaded with the members to throw their weight on the Spiritual side of the life of the church.[1]

He was listened to with care and at the next meeting it was resolved

> that this meeting expresses its opinions that the special element is amply provided for by the Annual meetings now being held and one social per month in addition and it is now very undesirable that the number be increased.[2]

The Reverend H.C. Morton was an important figure in the so-called 'quietist' movement which had recently emerged in Methodism, and indeed in British nonconformity as a whole, and which had been summed up in H.W. Clarke's book *Nonconformity and Politics* published three years earlier. In this Clarke, a Congregational minister, argued that nonconformity had become too involved in the non-spiritual side of life, especially in politics, and that while nonconformity 'has been making numerous and ardent

---

[1] East Sussex Record Office (ESRO) NMB 15/5/3. Leaders' Meeting Minutes, Eastbourne Wesleyan Methodist Chapel, Pevensey Road, 9 January 1912

[2] *Ibid.*, 16 April 1912

politicians, it has made scarcely any Saints'.[3]

Two things should be said straight away. Morton was a particular figure, a nationally known and able publicist for his view of Christianity. Nevertheless, I think he was representative of important strands within the Methodist body as a whole. Secondly, what he said, and indeed what Clarke and others said, was not particularly new. It was simply the latest manifestation of a split between quietism and politics which had ever been a part of religious Dissent. From its origins in the late sixteenth and seventeenth centuries there had been fierce battles between those moderates who wished to 'render unto Caesar' and those more radical figures who believed in, and fought for, the establishment of the new Jerusalem and the thousand year rule of the Saints. Part of John Wesley's great strength was, as Bernard Semmel argued some years ago, to bring both these elements together in a synthesis.

> The French and the Methodist Revolutions were calls both to a democratic revolution, though on different levels, and to order ... The call to order in Methodism was articulated at every point with the call for a spiritual revolution by a leader who was at once a revolutionary and the most rabid opponent of disorder.[4]

Within a few years of his death that 'synthesis' was shattered when the 'New Connexion' of Alexander Kilham (the so-called 'Tom Paine Methodist') was expelled from the Conference and this was followed in 1811 by the expulsion of the much more important followers of Henry Bourne and William Clowes, the Primitive Methodists.

But it is with the later nineteenth century that I shall be concerned here and mainly with East Anglia, for in the years between the 1860s and 1920s we can see with particular clarity some of the tensions which racked the 'chapel' and observe in some detail the struggle between politics and quietism.

The 'Social History' in the title of this paper may require some explanation. Social history was famously attacked as 'history with the politics left out' and here we have a paper which puts politics and social

---

[3] H.W. Clarke, 'A Nonconformist Minister', *Nonconformity and Politics*, 1909, p.130

[4] Bernard Semmel, *The Methodist Revolution*, 1974, p.196

history together in one phrase. I would like to quote from the sociologist C. Wright Mills.

> Know that many personal troubles cannot be solved merely as troubles, but must be understood in terms of public issues - and in terms of the problems of history making. Know that the human meaning of public issues must be revealed by relating them to personal troubles and to the problems of individual life. Know that the problems of social science, when adequately formulated, must include both troubles and issues, both biography and history, and the range of their intricate relations. Within that range the life of the individual and the making of society occur ...[5]

In other words a real history of any organisation has to be a social history because it brings together into Mills' 'intricate relations', the 'human documents', the accounts of the everyday and the ordinary, with the structures, the 'public issues'.

To begin with the public issues: the origins of many religious organisations of the nonconformist kind lie in a sense of exclusion, as Niebuhr noted many years ago about the late seventeenth-century American church and this also applies to nineteenth-century England.

> Whenever Christianity has become the religion of the fortunate and cultured and has grown philosophical, abstract, formal and ethically harmless in the process, the lower strata of society find themselves religiously expatriated by a faith which neither meets their psychological need nor sets forth an appealing ethical idea.[6]

It is not hard to see the Church of England in various phases of its faith in this way; equally it was and is possible to see aspects of nonconformity in this light. This was certainly the view of Philip Doddridge, the eighteenth-century Congregationalist divine who looked at his own modestly comfortable but declining congregations and wrote:

---

[5] Quoted in Ken Plummer, *Documents of Life. An Introduction to the Problems and Literature of a Humanistic Method*, 1990, p.4

[6] H. Richard Niebuhr, *The Social Sources of Denominationalism*, Cleveland and New York, 1956, p.33

[Soon] we shall have the greatest pleasure of being entertained with the echo of our own voices, and the delicacy of our discourses, in empty places, or amidst a little circle of friends, till, perhaps (like some of our brethren) we are starved into a good opinion of conformity.[7]

In this situation new groups emerge and break away from the parent body. To quote Niebuhr again:

In Protestant history the sect has ever been the child of the outcast minority, taking its rise in the religious revolts of the poor, of those who were without effective representation in church or state and who formed their conventicles of Dissent in the only way open to them, on the democratic, associational pattern.[8]

They were often born in anger, rejected and opposed by those around them, especially the groups from which they had split. Not for nothing did the first printed preaching plan of the Primitive Methodists contain the reproachful but proud quote from Acts xxviii 22: 'But we desire to hear of thee what thou thinkest: for as concerning this sect, we know that everywhere it is spoken against.' The sociologist Bryan Wilson has written how

change in the economic position of a particular group (or) disturbances of normal social relations are possible stimuli to the emergence of sects. These are needs to which sects, to some extent, respond. Particular groups are rendered marginal by some process of social change; there is a sudden need for a new interpretation of their social position or for a transvaluation of their experience.[9]

This is precisely what happened in the mid and late eighteenth century to a new semi-urban and industrial poor, the groups to whom Wesley spoke. In a less dramatic way it was what was happening in some rural districts of England after 1830. In the years between 1800 and 1830 rural England went through a major crisis caused by a rapid growth in population which was not

---

[7] Quoted in A.D. Gilbert, *Religion and Society in Industrial England*, 1976, p.16

[8] Niebuhr, *op.cit.*, p.19

[9] B.R. Wilson, 'An Analysis of Sect Development' in ed. Bryan R. Wilson, *Patterns of Sectarianism*, 1967, p.31

matched by any increase in economic opportunities. In a profoundly unequal society the poor pressed on the traditional organs of help like the Poor Law and private charity and found them wanting. Added to this the modification and decline of living-in farm service, continued enclosure and the increasingly casual nature of much rural employment pressed hard on those who remained in work. But it was not only an economic problem. It was a problem of belief. Charity and the Poor Laws were seen by the poor not as a gift, but as a right, due to them by custom and by Act of Parliament in return for their compliance with the social order. The removal of these traditional forms of help, particularly the replacement of the old Poor Law in 1834, represented a break in trust which lay at the heart of social relationships. William Cobbett saw this clearly when he wrote that if you did away with the old Poor Law, with its notional right to full relief, 'you dissolve the social compact as far as it relates to working people; without protection on one side there can be no right to protection on the other.'[10]

This breakdown in social relations particularly affected the Church of England which had always had a key role both in private charity and in the Poor Law. The parson who cared more for his tithes and his port, who lived in an Oxbridge College while drawing the stipend from three or four parishes, and who only appeared to sit on the bench or the Board of Guardians to 'oppress the poor and needy' became a central figure in the popular culture of the poor, even if the reality was sometimes different. James Ewing Ritchie, the radical Suffolk journalist, wrote of his boyhood in Benacre near Lowestoft.

> The churches round were mostly filled by the [landlord's] relatives, who came into possession of the family livings as a matter of course, and took little thought for the souls of their parishioners ... while the neighbouring gentry and all the parsons round, I am sorry to say, set the people a very bad example.[11]

Thus economic change, and its associated social changes, created the idea (and often the reality) of the Church of England as simply the religion of the élite.

---

[10] *Political Register*, 12 July 1874

[11] *Christopher Crayon's Recollections: the Life and Times of the late James Ewing Ritchie. As told by himself,* 1898, pp.37-8

POLITICS OR QUIETISM

Its close identification with the gentry and the aristocracy, particularly in the country districts, separated it from the poor. It was, however, also the church's religious failings which provoked the backlash against it in rural areas after 1830.

Think again of Niebuhr's phrase: the poor are 'expatriated', driven out of their own country, of their own churches. This is a social action, but it is also a religious one. A church may exclude by charging pew rents, by demanding social acceptability or by physically reproducing in its seating and organisation the inequalities of the outside world. It may also exclude by the irrelevance or antagonism of its teaching to a section of those who attend. We are back then to Mills' set of 'intricate relations' between the biography of individuals, the public sphere of economic, social and religious change, and the social relations of different groups.

To begin looking at these intimate relations let us look at two men. Both were born in Norfolk and lived most of their lives here, both were farm labourers and both were Primitive Methodists. Many readers will be familiar with the life of George Edwards.[12] Edwards was born in October 1850 at Marsham near Aylsham. His father was a farm worker and brickmaker, trades which Edwards followed, working at brickmaking in the summer and on the land in the winter. In March 1869 he was converted by a Primitive Methodist preacher called Samuel Harrison at Alby. He married in June 1872 and became a lay preacher for the Primitive Methodists in October of that year. In May 1872 he joined Joseph Arch's National Agricultural Labourers' Union and became branch secretary. In 1890 he became a full-time organiser for a new federal union - the Norfolk and Norwich Amalgamated Labourers' Union. When this union collapsed in 1896 he returned to the farm and to brickmaking. In 1906, with the financial aid of a group of wealthy East Anglian Liberals, he was instrumental in refounding a farmworkers' trade union. He was its secretary from then until 1913 when he retired and became its President. In 1920 he stood as Labour candidate for South Norfolk and won. Although he lost his seat in the General Election of 1922 he won it back in 1923. He retired in 1929 and died in Fakenham in 1933.

Many readers will also know the second man, George Rix.[13] He was

---

[12] For Edwards see George Edwards, *From Crow Scaring to Westminster*, 1922

[13] For Rix see 'The Life Story of George Rix of Swanton Morley told by Himself', *Eastern Weekly Press*, 7 April 1906, 14 April 1906, 21 April 1906

from an earlier generation, born at Bylaugh in November 1827. He started work, like Edwards, 'crow keeping' at ten years of age and graduated via looking after sheep to horse work by the time he was sixteen. He was married in 1849 and two years later became a higgler driving a dickey cart around the countryside north and east of Dereham. His mother was an early convert to Primitive Methodism and he followed in her footsteps, becoming a lay preacher in 1851 or 1852. In the same year he moved to Elsing where he bought land to build a chapel of which he became a trustee and Sunday School teacher. In the 1860s he moved to Swanton Morley and opened a small shop. About this time he became secretary of the North Tuddenham Friendly Benefit Society. In 1872 he was one of the founders of the National Agricultural Labourers' Union in Norfolk but split with Arch in 1878 on anti-centralist lines and founded the Norfolk Federal Union which became part of the Norfolk and Norwich Amalgamated in 1890. He was elected in 1889 as a 'working-man' candidate on the first Norfolk County Council from which he retired in 1897. He died at Swanton Morley in 1916.

These brief sketches are both religious and political biographies, so let us start by reading them more carefully, building on them to see how they fit into the 'intricate relations' of politics and quietism. Both men came to their religion at a time when Primitive Methodism was still 'everywhere spoken against', at least in East Anglia. Significantly, and we will return to this, Edwards was a convert while Rix was 'born' to the religion. Edwards was quite clear about his conversion and his account of this experience relates closely to the kinds of social-structural problems already discussed. His family's and his own experiences had freed him from any illusions about the nature of the ruling élite. He had no interest in the established church which seemed to him simply to reproduce the values and ideas which had condemned his family to the workhouse when his father was imprisoned for stealing turnips from a field. Immediately prior to his conversion he had

> begun to adopt rather bad habits ... I had taken to catching rabbits and selling them for pocket money. I had also begun to visit public houses ...[14]

Such behaviour is a common feature of biographies of this period and the subsequent conversion also followed familiar lines. It was emotional,

---

[14] Edwards, *op.cit.*, p.29

traumatic and totally transforming. At its most extreme such conversion experiences, especially when public, moved outside the bounds of Victorian good taste and set the convert and the preacher at odds with society. Joseph Barker, himself a Methodist and later a preacher, wrote of revival in the 1840s:

> Their manner of proceeding was truly dreadful. They jumped over the forms, climbed over the pews, kneeled down and prayed besides such as they supposed to be penitents, whispered in their ears, urged them to believe, talked in sterner ways to such as they supposed to be unawakened, thundered in their ears the horrors of damnation and eternal wrath, scores of them joining together to raise the wild excitement to its highest pitch.[15]

Such scenes were not unknown in Norfolk especially during Robert Key's missions in the county a few years earlier. In Sparham, for instance, a woman 'in much distress' came forward and, Key writes,

> I told her to kneel down, and God would save her in less than two minutes ... I had uttered but a few sentences ere she fell to the floor and in a few seconds sprang up shouting 'Victory, through the blood of the Lamb. Blessed be the name of our God for another glorious triumph over Satan.'[16]

Enthusiasm of this kind set those involved apart from Victorian society and this was often compounded by the fact that conversion could often change a person very dramatically. Zachariah Everett, a poacher converted while in Norwich Castle gaol, celebrated his release by preaching in Chapel Fields. He was rewarded by having his family turn up to mock him; his mother claimed that he had gone mad.[17] George Edwards' conversion at the hands of Samuel Harrison lacked this kind of intensity. He simply 'became very thoughtful and most strict in my habits.'[18] All converts, however, moved into a new world, the world of Chapel. To the saved, the world was a place

---

[15] *The Life of Joseph Barker written by himself*, edited by his nephew John Thomas Barker, 1880, pp.186-7

[16] Robert Key, *The Gospel Among the Masses*, 1872, p.30

[17] Zachariah Everett, *A Sketch of the Life of Z. Everett, a notorious poacher*, Norwich, 1867

[18] Edwards, *op. cit.*, p.30

of snares and temptation, the Godly needed to be ever on their guard, and their beliefs needed constant support. The individual could be isolated at work, in his or her village or even in his or her family. As Ritchie wrote:

> At one time I looked on myself as an outcast. With the Old Psalmist - with brave Oliver Cromwell - with generations of tried souls, I had to sing, as scotch Presbyterians, I believe, in Northern kirks still sing:
>
>> Woe's me that I in Meshec am
>> A sojourner so long,
>> Or that I in the tents do dwell
>> To Kedar that belong.[19]

To those who felt like this, chapel was a refuge and in the words of Watts' great hymn

> We are a Garden wall'd around,
> Chosen and made peculiar ground;
> A little spot inclos'd by Grace
> Out of the World's wide wilderness.

To the member this 'garden wall'd around' could, and often did constitute a whole way of life, a whole culture. It gave meaning, structure and discipline by institutionalising what Niebuhr calls the 'typical virtues of the class'.

> Hence one finds here, more than elsewhere, appreciation of the religious worth of solidarity and equality, of sympathy and mutual aid, of rigorous honesty in matters of debt, and the religious evaluation of simplicity in dress and manner, of the wisdom hidden to the wise and prudent but revealed to babes, of poverty of spirit, of humility and meekness.[20]

All these elements are present in the social formation of 'chapel' and in the world of Edwards and George Rix, Niebuhr's 'solidarity ... and mutual aid' finds a direct expression time and again in the formal and informal structures of chapel life. George Rix, for instance, after his election in 1875 as President

---

[19] *Christopher Crayon, op.cit.*, pp.57-8

[20] Niebuhr, *op.cit.*, p.31

of the North Tuddenham Friendly Benefit Society, proudly told the readers of the *Eastern Weekly Press* that he had been 'a member ... for upwards of thirty years, on the committee for many years; (and) one of the auditors for several years.'[21] The North Tuddenham Society, which was still known locally as the 'Ranters Club' up to the Great War, had been founded in 1834 specifically for the support of Primitive Methodist lay preachers. It seems to have opened its doors to anybody in the 1850s, but remained closely linked both by personnel and by its meeting places and by its temperance principles with the Primitive Methodists. Elsewhere chapels and Sunday School rooms provided many of the national orders with meeting places.[22] Chapel minute books reveal other less formal structures of solidarity and mutual aid. Clothing clubs, for instance, where members paid in small amounts each week to buy clothing once a year were important, as were slate clubs and the more formal 'penny banks'. Many chapels also had a range of less structured systems of aid. At Eastbourne in 1889, for example, a Mr J. Allen was given £2 from the Poor Fund 'to assist him to Australia' while three years later a member who had migrated to Wales was 'sent 5s because of his temporary need.'[23]

The other side of this mutual aid was discipline. Chapel society stressed public and private decency to a level which now seems extreme. What Niebuhr sees as the 'moral values resident in the necessities' of the life of the poor were elevated to what was on occasions an almost obsessive concern with debt, drunkenness, public demeanour and, in particular, sexual behaviour. Lewes Circuit regularly looked at the financial status of its preachers and members and removed names from the plan if and when they transgressed the bounds of chapel morality. In 1884 one 'Brother Stephens' had his name removed because of his 'Embarrassed position financially'.[24] A few years later Mr Peart was asked to resign because 'he had been unable to meet the demands of his creditors.'[25] Sabbatarianism was perhaps more

[21] *Eastern Weekly Press*, 22 May 1875

[22] ESRO NMB 15/1/2, Trustees' Minutes, Eastbourne Pevensey Road, 30 October 1907

[23] ESRO NMB 15/5/1, Minutes of Leaders' Meetings, Eastbourne Pevensey Road, 18 September 1889; 25 April 1892

[24] ESRO NMA 1/9/1, Lewes Wesleyan Methodist Circuit Minutes, 2 July 1884

[25] ESRO NMA 1/7/1, *ibid.*, 30 March 1897

understandable, but it could cause serious problems as at Haywards Heath in Sussex where two members were expelled for opening their small shop on a Sunday, even though Sunday opening was vital to their livelihood and they were in all other respects exemplary members.[26]

Drink, although not formally banned until the 1860s, was always seen as a problem and many members found here, as elsewhere, that membership of chapel excluded them from normal places of popular culture. George Edwards, as we have seen, saw drink as one of the signs of his former degeneration and George Rix boasted that one of the great strengths of the North Tuddenham Friendly Society was that it did not meet in public houses. By the 1860s, being seen in a public house was reason enough for expulsion as Brothers Smith and Ward of Mattishall in Norfolk found in 1868 when they were warned for having attended 'a Meeting at a Public House where there were Music, Song singing and dancing and where they remained until past 12 o'clock.'[27] Family relationships and sexual conduct was also judged and frequently found wanting, although in parts of Britain, especially Wales and the West Country, nonconformity proved remarkably adaptable to local custom. In Norfolk we find members in trouble for not living together as couples, for violence within the family and for 'immorality'[28]

In part because of their assurance of salvation and in part because of their changed behaviour, chapel members were increasingly excluded from the places of working class and popular culture. As a result they began to create for themselves an alternative world, a sub-culture which embraced much of their lives. By the 1880s most chapels offered some form of social or religious activity on every night of the week as well as during most of Sunday. Prayer meetings, revival services, Wesley Guild, slate clubs, Women's and Men's meetings, class meetings, missionary lectures, services of song, class meetings as well as a big annual 'do' like the anniversary meetings and bazaars, and the Sunday commitment to two services and Sunday School meant that a chapel member could be cocooned in a separate world. This was reinforced by the

---

[26] ESRO NMA 1/24/1, Haywards Heath Primitive Methodist Mission Quarterly Meetings, 8 September 1892

[27] East Dereham Primitive Methodist Circuit Minutes, 16 September 1868. In the possession of Mr C. Jolly

[28] *Ibid.*, 16 December 1867; 15 June 1868; 3 June 1882

fact that informal social contact was often restricted to other chapel members. Oral sources tell time and again of such things - 'pie suppers' organised by a group of chapel families and paid for collectively; here and there a melodeon or concertina abandoned the Devil's tunes and played the sacred songs and solos of Sankey and Moody. Sunday afternoons and early evenings after chapel, especially in the summer, were a time for visiting, and for all but the most strict Sabbatarians were again a time for song and sacred readings.[29]

'What went on in chapel' became not only the subject of purient tales and jokes (especially the Primitive Methodists' very chaste 'Love Feasts') but of more worried political speculation. In the Chilterns in the 1840s, 'it had been rumoured that these prayer-meetings were more political than religious.'[30] More widespread was the fact that a simple challenge to theological orthodoxy and religious control provoked boycotting of shops, dismissal from work and social ostracism. However, the culture of chapel contained within it a much more potent threat. Methodism, and particularly Primitive Methodism, relied very heavily on lay preachers. To become a preacher needed education, albeit of a basic kind. George Edwards saw this. In 1872 he was accepted onto the plan as an 'exhorter' and he wrote:

> Up to this point I could not read, I merely knew my letters, but I set myself to work. My dear wife came to my rescue and undertook to teach me to read. For the purpose of this first service she helped me to commit three hymns to memory and also the first chapters of the Gospel according to St John ... When I returned home from work after tea she would get a hymn book, read the lines out, and I would repeat them after her.

Learning to read, learning to speak in public or to run a meeting created a much more 'political' world. The Reverend Augustus Jessop of Scarning noted that it created

---

[29] Essex University Oral History Collection. Interviews with Mr Jaggard, Great Bentley, Essex; Mr Rush, Reading; Mr Tanner, Keighley

[30] John Buckmaster, *A Village Politician: the Life Story of John Buckley*, new ed., Horsham, 1982, p.30

a school of eloquence, in which the lowliest has become familiarized with the ordinary rules of debate, and has been trained to express himself with directness, vigour and fluency.[31]

But it did more than that. George Edwards put it starkly,

> with my study of theology, I soon began to realise that the social conditions of the people were not as God intended they should be.[32]

This personal leap was an intensely private feeling at first, but led on to an understanding of local political situations. It was, initially at least, very different from the motives of people like Edward Miall who led national political campaigns and created the notion of the 'nonconformist conscience' in national politics. Although people like Edwards and Rix supported these campaigns, they did so at a distance as the rank-and-file. This meant that while they were deeply involved in local manifestations of the national campaigns, it was in their localities that they felt the real battles were fought.

The key here was trade unionism. This is not the place to go over that ground again in any detail, but simply to highlight a few particular areas. First, nearly all unions in East Anglia and elsewhere began locally. Despite the grandiose claims of Joseph Arch, very few districts where the union had any permanent strength were missioned from outside by his NALU. Most were led by local men and often focused on particular local grievances. Second, once the unions were established they constantly clashed with the centre on the question of local autonomy. George Rix and George Edwards both opposed the excessive centralism of the NALU from the late 1870s and Rix split with Arch in 1878 to form the Norfolk Federal Union. The Norfolk experience was summed up in a letter to the *Eastern Weekly Press* from 'An Old Member of the Labourers' Unions' addressed to Joseph Arch.

> We shall not forsake our long-tried and proved leaders to please your whims

---

[31] Augustus Jessop, *Arcardy for Better or Worse*, 1887, p.77
[32] Edwards, *op.cit.*, p.36

and fancies ... we have summered and wintered them ... Long before we heard of your existence ... we would rather a thousand times forsake you than our present faithful leaders.[33]

Third, the issues in which chapel and union men were involved in the 1870s and 1880s were nearly all local. Battles like the Scarning Free School Dispute, the Mattishall and Reepham 'enclosure' fights and the various struggles over village charities had a distinctly local focus. It is noteworthy that when George Rix was elected to the first Norfolk County Council in 1889 he stood not as a Liberal but as a 'working-man's candidate'.

From the union's beginnings in Norfolk the local leadership was dominated by Primitive Methodists, many of whom were lay preachers and even chapel trustees. As a result, chapel buildings were frequently used for union meetings. The first meeting at Wymondham, for instance, was held in the Primitive chapel 'kindly lent by the trustees, who considered that it would be a more suitable place for their discussions than a room at an Inn'.[34] The language and meaning of the Bible were also frequently invoked in the union's cause. Henry Gibson who spoke at the first meeting in Dereham began by reading the first psalm ('Blessed is the man that walketh not in the counsel of the ungodly ...) and afterwards prayed to God 'that if the Union were of man it might fail but if it were of Him it might flourish'.[35]

The social world of chapel remained, however, primarily religious and those who took from it both a social gospel and a strength to create a new Jerusalem were not the only voices. Even in the almost millennial year of 1872 there were those in Primitive Methodism who opposed the union's use of chapel buildings. At North Lopham in November 1872 the trustees refused the union the use of the school room and chapel, a decision which was supported by both the Circuit Superintendent and by the Quarterly meeting.[36] By 1873 even the union's heartland, the East Dereham Circuit in which George Rix was a preacher and a key member, moved to stop the union using its chapels. In March that year a complaint was received at the

---

[33] *Eastern Weekly Press*, (*EWP*) 8 February 1879
[34] *Ibid.*, 4 May 1872
[35] *Ibid.*, 11 January 1873
[36] *Ibid.*, 14 December 1872

Quarterly meeting against 'those brothers' using 'our chapels' for agricultural labourers' meetings. Rix and his supporters tried to sidestep the issue by claiming that the union was non-political and by referring the question of whether or not it was political to the General Secretary. In the meantime where a majority of the trustees was in favour the chapel could continue to be used. In April the reply came back from the centre that 'it is illegal for [the union] to hold meetings in our chapels' and instructed them to stop. However Rix and others argued that the question had been whether or not the union was political and this had not been answered. They carried the day, and as a result chapels continued to be used where a majority of trustees was in favour.[37]

This did, however, cause some problems. At Bawdeswell the principle members of the Primitive Methodist chapel were farmers and no admission was allowed to the union delegates, even though both were local Primitive Methodist preachers. But, fortunately for the union, 'the Reform Wesleyans are not so timid on this question' and their chapel was used thereafter for union meetings in the village.[38] Some of this argument was in public, with Rix insisting on the 'Christian standpoint' of the union. This was too much even for the East Dereham Circuit and eventually in 1879 Rix was reprimanded for making public its internal arguments.[39] More hostility came from outside the Primitives when A.J.N. Chamberlain, an early supporter of the union and a Wesleyan preacher, associated himself with the Norfolk Farmers' Labour Defence Association in their attacks on the union. Chamberlain, however, seems to have been no more than the public tip of a larger iceberg since Rix felt compelled to answer him and ended by saying that 'hundreds' of Dissenting parsons 'had been amongst their worst opponents.'[40]

Chamberlain's attack on the union seems to have been from a fairly standard anti-union position, but others took a more complicated stance. Some of those on the East Dereham Circuit who did not want the union to use chapels were clearly not anti-union. It was rather that they did not see

---

[37] East Dereham Minutes, *op.cit.*, 17 March 1873; 14 April 1873; 16 June 1873

[38] *Ibid.*, 9 June 1879

[39] *Ibid.*, 23 March 1874 - 6 June 1874

[40] *Ibid.*, 16 May 1874

that a religious organisation should have this kind of political role. Temperance, the defence of Christian communities abroad, Church rates, even disestablishment were political issues on which the chapel did and should have a position. Industrial and social strife was a very different matter. Gradually at first (and this can only be impressionistic) meetings seem to have been held less and less in chapels. In 1874 the Norwich District, unlike East Dereham, banned the holding of union meetings in chapels completely despite a fierce public debate in the press. The District argued that the chapels had been built by all members of the communities in which they stood, and especially by the farmers, and that the union was, by its intemperate language, in effect preaching some kind of class war and dividing villages against themselves.[41] It was, however, probably more often the case that, as at Bawdeswell and Lyng, the trustees of individual chapels simply objected to the meetings being held on their premises.

There is some evidence for moves within chapels to control what the 'labour' preachers were saying in sermons and addresses. There is, for example, a suggestion that in the 1880s some of Rix's sermons were considered too radical, and Edwards certainly seems to have suffered from a concerted attempt to control what he said. In the late 1880s he was summoned before the Quarterly meeting of the Cromer Circuit

> ... for what some of the elder brethren term hetrodoxical preaching and I was regarded almost as an infidel.[42]

By 1895 things seem to have gone further and he said at a public meeting in Cromer,

> I will admit at once that the nonconformists have not moved along these few years so fast as some of the more ardent spirits amongst us could have wished, and they have far too much ignored the fact that Christ came to redress social wrongs as much as to prepare the way for a higher life.[43]

Here was the crux of the growing quietist criticism. The social gospel, it was

---

[41] *Ibid.*, 23 May 1874

[42] Edwards, *op.cit.*, p.52

[43] *Eastern Weekly Leader*, 2 February 1895

increasingly argued, was inappropriate. In a long article in the *Eastern Weekly Leader* at the end of 1895 Edwards wrote of a conversation with a 'friend' who 'had heard that I had severed all connections with Christian societies'. The friend puts it to Edwards that as Christians they should 'first seek the Kingdom of God and His righteousness' before any secular concern. Edwards replies that the Kingdom of God 'was a state where equality reigned supreme, and where the grand principle of brotherhood was carried on in its entirety.' It was, he continued, precisely because the chapels and churches refused to preach a social gospel and allowed its

> truth to be perverted that they were so empty. Until the Christian Church endeavours to get our social evils rectified, and brings the mass of the people on a more equal footing, they will never succeed in bringing men to God.[44]

The article should have been a clarion cry, but it was the opposite. Although Edwards remained loyal to the Primitive Methodist cause he was increasingly alienated from it. By 1907 he asserted that he had been 'boycotted' from many chapels because of his advanced views[45] and he continued to have difficulties with the chapel up to the outbreak of the Great War. In 1895, moreover, the 'first' union finally collapsed taking with it many of the hopes of the golden age of Norfolk radical nonconformity; for when the union returned in 1906 it was, in several respects, a very different animal. We can see some of the reasons for this in our human documents, especially here in George Rix. Rix was, as we said right at the beginning, born into Methodism. Niebuhr has argued that those born into a sect are different from those converted to it.

> For with their coming the sect must take on the character of an educational and disciplinary institution, with the purpose of bringing the new generation to conformity with the ideals and customs which have become traditional. Rarely does a second generation hold the convictions it has inherited with a fervour equal to that of its fathers, who fashioned these convictions in the heat of conflict and at the risk of martyrdom.[46]

---

[44] *Ibid.*, 14 September 1895

[45] *EWP*, April 1907

[46] Niebuhr, *op.cit.*, pp.19-20

Now that judgement is only partly true of Rix, but it does highlight a more general truth about radical nonconformity by the 1890s. No longer was Primitive Methodism 'everywhere spoken against'. It had MPs, its Connexional History printed in 1911 was an impressive two-volume work which testified to the Prims' centrality in English nonconformity and in English life. Above all its members and its chapels had become a respectable part of the local establishment albeit in a minor way. Rix saw this when, in 1876, he told a court with some pride that he had 'property in Elsing which cost me for land and building £200 and other property where I live',[47] and boasted in old age of how his chapel principles ('bein' a strictly temperance and no smoking man') enabled him to save and to build up a 'good livin' business.'[48]

Wesley had said, 'the Methodists in every place grow diligent and frugal and hence they increase their goods', but it was, in reality, a much wider-based reassertion of the spiritual as opposed to the social aspects of Christianity. It was not only the direct local contacts with politics that decreased, but a whole range of 'secular' aspects of the church's life. Thus, for example, in the late 1870s and early 1880s Benefit Societies came under threat. As George Rix wrote somewhat bitterly,

> This is another fresh proof of the difficulties to be encountered in establishing and carrying on every course that has for its object the temporal welfare of the hard working and deserving working man. It is a blot on Methodism.[49]

Nor did the social Christianity of Hugh Price Hughes and the great Central Halls movement have much effect in the rural areas, unless it was to indirectly unite all Methodists in the belief that the main problems lay elsewhere, in an urban setting. Equally seriously, as Bebbington says, the

> emergence of the Labour Party raised the spectre of acute internal controversy in Nonconformity and so discouraged the public airing of political views.[50]

---

[47] *EWP*, 14 April 1906
[48] *Ibid.*, 11 November 1899
[49] *Ibid.*, 19 April 1879
[50] D.W. Bebbington, *The Nonconformist Conscience*, 1982, p.158

When the labourers' union reappeared in 1906 these changes were clearly apparent. Gone was the millenarian language of the 1870s. Few if any called on God to bless their proceedings even at the founding meeting. More importantly, although many trades unionists and radicals of the 1900s and even 1920s spent their formative years in the chapel, the direct link between chapel organisation and union was gone; it is significant that no meetings of the second union were held in chapels.

In Norfolk and elsewhere, as Bebbington suggests, the emergence of Labour caused problems. In many militant areas, like the mining areas of county Durham written about by Robert Moore, it split the chapel absolutely.[51] In Norfolk it was less dramatic, but problems there were. In 1907, for instance, the trustees of Sprowston chapel refused its use to the Independent Labour Party during the Norwich municipal elections despite the latter's insistence that 'they wanted a brotherhood that would bring about the Kingdom of God'.[52] Eventually George Edwards was to join the ILP and in 1913 the farmworkers' union affiliated to the Labour Party. We are in a sense back to the beginning - to the spiritual church wanted by the Revd Morton at Eastbourne. It has recently become fashionable among certain nonconformist historians like Donald Davie to argue that radical nonconformity was a sham, that it only ever embraced a few and that it probably did more harm than good. I would disagree. The nonconformist culture of rural areas in the late nineteenth century, like others before it, was a powerful and persuasive one. When it changed, it left behind the poor, just as its antecedents had done. The difference was that it left them to a secular society; there was no new church of the disinherited to take its place. What Niebuhr wrote in the 1920s remains so still.

> There is no effective religious movement among the disinherited today; as a result they are simply outside the pale of organised Christianity.[53]

That is a very high price to pay for a spiritual and non-political religion.

---

[51] Robert Moore, *Pitmen, Preachers and Politics* Cambridge, 1974

[52] *EWP* 8 November 1907

[53] Niebuhr, *op.cit.*, p.76

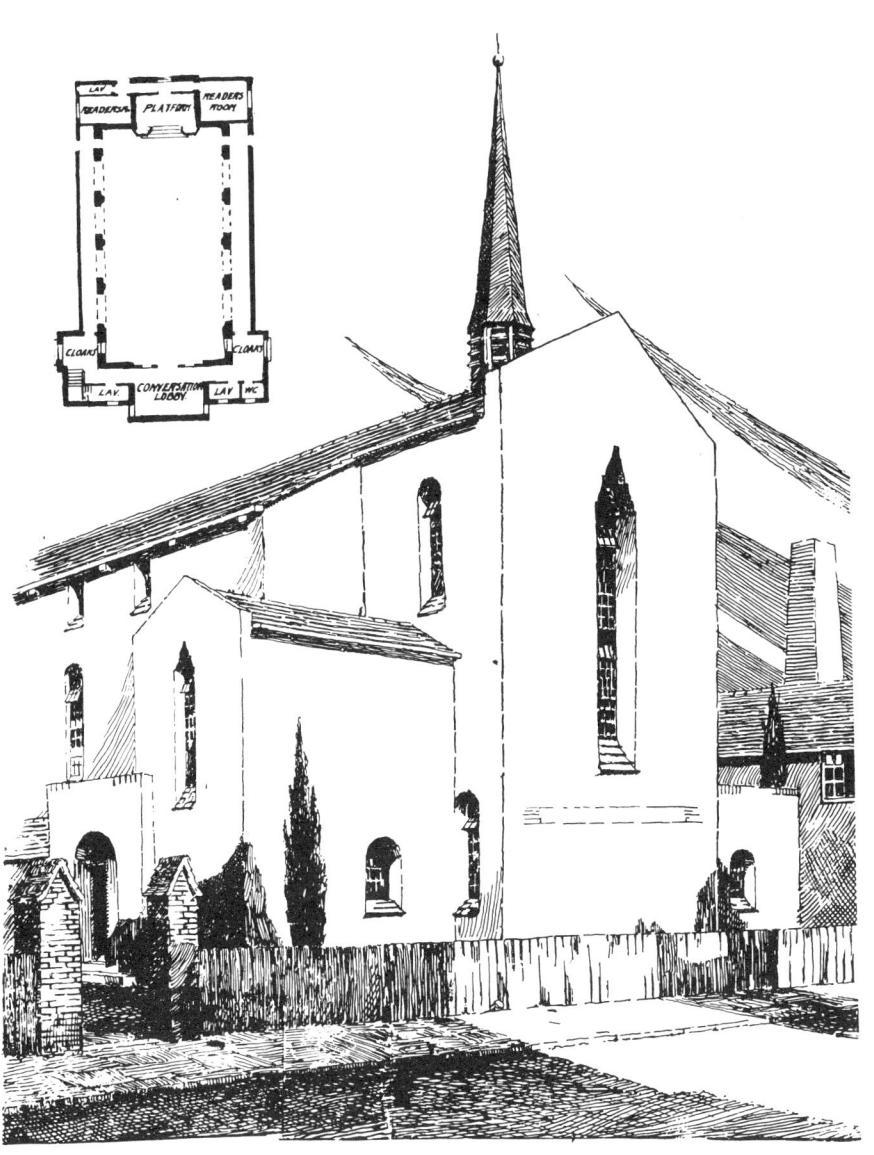

The First Church of Christ, Scientist, Recorder Road, Norwich (1935)

AN EXCURSION INTO ARCHITECTURAL COUSINHOOD: THE EAST ANGLIAN CONNEXION[1]

CLYDE BINFIELD

I

Norwich's most distinctive, and perhaps most complete, nonconformist church — the Octagon apart — is among its least known. It is the Christian Science Church on Recorder Road. Christian Science is not in the nonconformist mainstream; Recorder Road is a side street; and the 1930s, when this church was built, are seldom seen as a prime time for chapel architecture. In the eyes of Christian Scientists, too, this building is something of a sport since it is noticeably more 'churchy' than most of their premises.

It is worth more than a second look. Outside it is the ultimate in stripped gothic, given away church-wise by its loftiness and the flêche surmounting an oak ventilation shaft. That copper spirelet may be a cliché but it is the passer-by's best clue. Although it is in Norfolk, the church is built in

---

[1] For help in the preparation of this paper I owe a variety of debts to Mr H. Godwin Arnold, Mr David Barton, Mr E. de C. Blomfield, Mr H.C. Boardman, Mr Michael Brooks, the Revd A.K. Bryan, the Revd Geoffrey Collins, Dr Morton Figgis, Mr Nigel Figgis, Mr Terence Figgis, Miss Dorothy Gardner, Dr Hilary Grainger, Mr G.C. Greatham, Miss Grace Gurteen, Mr W.E. Hall, Mr W. Heap, Mrs D.B.L. Hoegger, Mr C.I. Hooper, Mrs K.M. Hooper, The Revd Canon W.M. Jacob, Mr C.B. Jewson, Miss Nancy Jewson, Miss Ruth Kamen, *The Leicester Mercury*, Mrs S.M. Mills, Mr A.A. Smith, Mr Christopher Stell, Mr Aubrey Stevenson, the Revd J.H. Taylor, the Revd John Travell, Mrs Margaret Unthank, Dr & Mrs R. Virgoe, Mrs Muriel Wilshaw, Mrs Marjorie Wright. An earlier version of parts of this paper appeared in C. Binfield, 'Towards an Appreciation of Baptist Architecture', *Baptists in the Twentieth Century* ed. K.W. Clements, Baptist Historical Society, 1983 pp.114-42 esp. 129-37

wealden stock brick from Sussex and it has other jolly little Sussex touches. There are chequer-board squares of rough flint and scraps of excavated stone, as in the Sussex vernacular, and the putlog holes into which the scaffolding poles fitted have been filled with flint.

Inside, the floor is raked in good wood block. As in so many chapels there is something not quite right about the focal point — a platform set in a barrel-vaulted chancel. To either side, following Christian Science practice, are the readers' desks, higher than the architect first intended. On a pedestal, flanked by steps from floor to platform, is the bowl of flowers. Behind the platform, and with narrow openings at either side to the rear passage and the readers' rooms, is a plain partition supporting a plain gallery. On each wall beside the chancel recess is a text in incised lettering. 'Ye Shall Know the Truth and the Truth Shall Make You Free' faces the congregation's left side and 'Divine Love Always Has Met and Always Will Meet Every Human Need' faces its right. The former are words of Jesus, the latter of Mary Baker Eddy.

There are two first impressions. One is of height, accentuated by the aisles and their arches to each side. The other is of breadth, emphasised by the wooden ceiling. The next impressions are of artfulness and quietly insistent symbolism. If the shell is stripped gothic, the platform end is stripped Bible land. The windows on either side of the auditorium (how one wishes to say 'nave'), each one set in an arch above the aisles, are tall and thin and in plain glass, like white candles: for above each is a small clerestory window which could be the candle flame, with a golden pane glowing at its heart. This candle flame motif is repeated in the high, thin window fronting Recorder Road, in the window above the main side entrance, and again in the doors nearest the platform. The architect took care over his lighting, which was originally thrown from bowls on to the ceiling. He took care over other things: there is a ventilation niche in each clerestory arch; there are rush-seated chairs, with oak benches for the gallery.

The general plan shows a fine economy. You can enter the building from either side, with simple texts (God is Love; He Sent His Word and Healed Them) to help your frame of mind. Sensibly, you find yourself in a vestibule for coats, with a lavatory off it. Then you can go straight into the church or, if time permits, you can linger in the conversation lobby, with its leather-covered and studded doors. Either side of the doors leading into the auditorium are windows with leaded lights which have panes of deep blue glass at their centre. There is a gallery above the lobby. This is corked. Perhaps it was, or was intended to be, wood-panelled. Elsewhere the walls are natural roughcast. In the evening glow they take on a warm buff-beige; in hard daylight they look rather grubby.

How did all this get there? What chemistry made this Church of Christ Scientist? It was done very briskly by a Building Committee of five people, two of them women, between 5 September 1933 and 22 January 1935.[2]

The Members' Meeting of Norwich's First Church of Christ Scientist, very down town in Recorder Road, set up a committee 'to consider and report on all aspects of providing a larger Church'. That committee met on 5 September 1933 at 7 pm. It opened with readings from the Bible and the works of Mary Baker Eddy, followed by silent prayer and then the Lord's Prayer. It then dealt with procedure. There were two procedures: 'Metaphysical Procedure' and 'Building Procedure'. The Metaphysical Procedure was less alarming than it sounds: at each meeting the Chairman gave readings of his own choosing and a committee member followed, expounding on a subject determined at the previous meeting. The Buildings Procedure was entirely businesslike. On this occasion the chairman was to meet the city architect to see if 'the Town Planning scheme for the City would permit a church building to be erected on this site' and whether there were other suitable sites; the secretary was to write to the new church at Sutton in Surrey.

The committee met another twenty-seven times. On each occasion it began metaphysically with readings which were carefully, even ingenuously balanced: 'Choose ye' and 'Unity'; 'Spiritual Building' and 'The Carnal Mind's Methods'; 'Rise and Build' and 'Choosing an Architect'; 'Divine Plan' and 'Foundation'. There was a whole series on 'Funds' — 'Supply Infinite' (and 'Perception'); 'Abundance' (and 'No Delay'); 'Supply at Hand' (and 'Atmosphere'); later yet 'The Proof of Gratitude' (and 'Completeness'); then back to 'Supply' (with 'Chemicalization'); and so to 'Love Produces Supply' and 'Eternal Church'.

The practicalities were cleared providentially. The city surveyor could see no reason 'why a Church should not be built on the present site if in

---

[2] This section is based on First Church of Christ, Scientist, Norwich. 'Building Committee: Book of Minutes 5 September 1933 - 22 January 1935', in possession of the church. A Christian Science Society was first organised in Norwich in 1911. It became the First Church of Christ, Scientist, Norwich, with twenty-nine members, in April 1921. By then it was meeting in renovated stables in Recorder Road. *First Church of Christ, Scientist, Norwich, England*, brochure 26 July 1936.

conformity with the building laws of the City'. The problem of ancient lights with regard to the neighbouring motor garage proved to be no problem at all since the Norwich Motor Co Ltd Garage was far too new to have acquired any ancient lights. No other site seemed to meet the need, although there was a hiccup when news came that a dance hall was to be built at the end of the street and the committee was asked 'to do protective work'.

And the architect evolved. That is the only way to describe it. At the first meeting Mrs Jewson had a suggestion. Jewson is a name that resonates in twentieth-century Norwich. Herbert Jewson was an engineer. Mrs Herbert Jewson was reared a Congregationalist, had married into the strongly Baptist and formidably civic Jewson family and was now a much respected Christian Science practitioner and a stalwart of the cause in Recorder Road.[3] 'Mrs Jewson will ask Mr Ibberson, an architect who has designed several Nonconformist Churches to give us his views, in a friendly way, of the possibilities of our site.' Mr Ibberson did so at once and at the next meeting Jessie Jewson presented his rough plan for a church to seat 400 and to cost £6,000. It would be in a tawny grey brick, with a copper ventilator like a small spire. In all fundamental respects it was like the present building.

It was agreed that the church members should see this plan, but there were other possibilities. Each member of the committee had a bright and sensible idea, and it was thought that the new Christian Science Churches at Sutton and Bexhill might spark more ideas. Mr Ibberson, however, was a wise man. Through Mrs Jewson he recommended 'Mr Starkey, a C[hristian] S[cience] architect with whom he has collaborated'; and Mrs Jewson's choice for the next meeting's reading was 'the Carnal Mind's Methods'.

These other possibilities and other architects, however, did not come up to expectation and at the end of September it was formally resolved to submit Ibberson's designs and those of a local architect, Mr Scott, to the Board of the Church. Ibberson had provided alternative plans for a £6,000 church and a £4,000 one; Scott's were for a remodelling of the existing room at £1,200 and a semi-permanent scheme at £2,100. A letter was to go to the 'Trustees under the Will of Mrs Eddy' to see what they would grant towards a permanent building.

---

[3] Harriet Jessie Hewitt joined Clarendon Park Congregational Church, Leicester, 29 March 1893, moving to East Dereham, Norfolk in 1899 on her marriage to Herbert Jewson.

There matters stood for a while. On 9 January 1934, after the selected reading 'Choosing an Architect', the committee met to do just that. Four new names were now in the air and photographs and plans of two churches by A.P. Starkey were on the table. It was to no avail. 'Eventually it was suggested that we make no decision at the moment but put in some more work. We had talked things over thoroughly and it might be as well to put in some more time in claiming Divine guidance.'

That came on 23 January. Mrs Jewson read on 'Unity'. Plans were produced of a church in Canada, but it was unanimously agreed to recommend Mr Ibberson and the Building Committee was reconstituted. It now comprised six people, two of them women. Mrs Jewson was not on it. Perhaps that was as well. She had had her way; and Mr Ibberson was her brother-in-law.

The architect had evolved. Now his church was to follow suit. On 15 February fuller plans were examined; builders were agreed (without going to tender); heating was recommended ('Thermola' — a fan behind a radiator, keeping hot and cold air on the move; committee member Morgan had 'Thermola' in his factory). And an obstacle appeared: 'A hole had been dug in the church garden and water reached at a depth of 7 inches'. Not too tragic a view was taken of that.

Subsequent meetings worried over doors (swing or with oil stops?), heating, acoustics, colour of bricks, light from windows, placing of desks. May saw the lapse which is expected of any architect — Ibberson had drawn his plans on the assumption that the site was rectangular, and it was not. They managed somehow. The architect explained why the back passage had to be the height it was and why raising the rake of the floor would affect the height of the rear arch; and he would carve a text in wood over the door to the south lobby to words chosen by the Board: 'He sent His Word and healed them'. On 25 July 1934 the Date Stone was laid. The chairman had prepared a report of this, but his committee 'objected to the names of any of those taking part being mentioned'; and the 'Chairman spoke of circumstances which showed the need of protective work against division'.

On 4 September, a year almost to the day after the first meeting, the committee viewed its creation, found it good and agreed to send Ibberson a letter of appreciation. Life thereafter was a matter of dotting fabric i's and crossing architectural t's. The architect retained command of the choice of glass, but the choice of chairs was less easy. Three samples were viewed, but as Mr Morgan put it, he had a better type in his own home. And as in every chapel, when all was over, the draughts remained. Mr Morgan found the solution:

> *Draughts in Church* ... Mr Morgan advocated heating organ loft on the theory that the cold air is pulled down into the body of the Church by the hot air below, distressing the Readers as it passes them. Decided to put a fire in loft as an experiment.

The experiment worked; and the architect did not feel that fire extinguishers were necessary.

Warmth of another kind was provided in those early days at the platform end by 'coloured tapestry curtains as selected by Mr I. ... Texts to be selected by members. Texts to be in gold letters on blue ground panel on the curtains'. Those curtains have now gone and their texts are incised on the walls instead.

On 27 January 1935 the committee called it a day. Their church had cost £4,446, including extras and foundations. Of this £1,700 was still to be found. It was reported that 'Mr Ibberson and Mr Carter [the builder] had enjoyed their work'. It was Mr Ibberson's last major work; he died on 16 June 'without a moment's warning'.[4]

II

In this everyday story of Dissenting church building are to be found art and craftsmanship, fitness for purpose and apt patronage, widely networked and yet well-earthed in its locality. Place, polity and professionalism play their part. It brings a wide segment of English life and culture into focus. What follows explores that segment, informed by three concerns. The first is the

---

[4] JCH 'A Master Builder', cutting dated 29 June 1935, belonging to Revd A.K. Bryan. JCH went on to quote Ibberson - 'The Spirit of the Lord is with all these people, but their ways are strangely different. I am thinking of writing a tract on 'Comparative Committees'. The Baptists are great on teas; we lay stones with teas and open with more tea. The Vicar is roped in, with the chairman of the local council, and representatives of sister churches. Mrs Eddy had none of these material rejoicings, so her followers have none; nothing happens at the beginning or the end, except the usual 'testimony meeting'; no public thanks to builder or architect. But they wrote to me, officially, charming letters of thanks, not only at the end, but in the middle of the work.'

emergence of architects as professional men; or, rather, it is their emergence in thickening numbers at a time when other professionals are emerging. The second is the part played in this growth by men who happened to be Protestant nonconformists. The third gives purpose to this coincidence, for it is about Dissenting architects.

The emergence of an architectural profession, that is to say the formal structuring of proponents of the art of structure, is not surprising.[5] Its trigger is the boom not just in building but in a multiplicity of building types. Its context is the culture and politics which accompanied that boom. It is about building houses, the artisan's dwelling joining the villa, the semi-villa and the mansion, so that newly registered voters could live in them; schools, in a society where politics, shaped by religion, at once up-ended and retarded the entire system at every level from dame schools to university colleges; and hospitals, in a grudgingly health-conscious society. It is about building churches in a religious world whose complex polities offered unending scope for ingenious variation; commercial buildings, from corner shops and warehouses to department stores and office blocks; factories, whether mills or sheds; and railway stations. Holding these together are buildings for the new apparatus without which there would be chaos — town halls and vestry halls, home and colonial and foreign and war offices, school-board offices, church houses; and then more buildings still, hotels and clubs and pubs, for them all to relax in.

So far, so obvious. Less obvious is the cumulative interlocking of this. Churchmen, educationists, bureaucrats, politicians, health experts, became aware of overlapping needs. You cannot teach ill or starving children any more than you can preach to them or sell to them. For all the apparently ineradicable prejudice against blanket solutions, Englishmen found that the overview was forced on them in a society which was losing its boundaries. Their buildings express this to perfection. So, too, do the builder types responsible for these building types: builders and builders' merchants, property speculators and estate agents, auctioneers and surveyors, engineers, planners, valuers. Each merges into the next. From each emerges a component which issues in the *architect*, whose role is defined (but never exclusively) by the Institute of British Architects (1834; Royal from 1837),

---

[5] B. Kaye, *The Development of the Architectural Profession in Britain: a Sociological Study*, 1960

its mission mediated through the Architectural Association (1847), the whole fostered in a series of provincial societies. And somewhere in this emergence there is art, creativity, with its characteristics of taste and style, and craftsmanship of hand or machine.

How does religious Dissent fit into this? It is arguable that specifically Dissenting insights have influenced the development of a creative profession. More to the point is the fact that nonconformity is conformity's underside, poised in the English experience at the edge of the political nation, just within it by law, kept in its place too by law, as well as by custom; nonconformity, both articulate and sentient, at once irritable, cringing, awkward, meekly superior and honourably devious, full of growing pains. The emerging professions are tailor-made for bright young Dissenters. Dissent and the new professions are alike on edge, representing society as it might be and probably will be and up against society as it has for too long tended to be. In the Industrial Revolution's first swell Dissent made sense to uprooted artisans. It allowed them to control their world from the encouraging vantage point of eternity. Now that England was an ageing industrial nation and Dissenters had made their way in it, the new professions made sense to their posterity. You too could die like Sir Gilbert Scott, worth £130,000;[6] or disentangle medieval style like Thomas Rickman, who was a Quaker turned Irvingite;[7] or transmute the medieval spirit into modern need, like Alfred Waterhouse, whose origins were also Quaker.[8] You could be Aston Webb, whose father-in-law was a Congregational deacon,[9] or William Butterfield, whose formation — so unlike his maturity — lay in the evangelical world of Whitefieldite Tabernacles and Lady

---

[6] D. Cole, *The Work of Sir Gilbert Scott*, 1980 p.182. For Scott (1811-78) see also *Dictionary of National Biography*

[7] For Thomas Rickman (1776-1841) see *DNB*

[8] For Alfred Waterhouse (1830-1905) see *DNB* and *Seven Victorian Architects*, 1976, ed. Jane Fawcett, 1976

[9] For Sir Aston Webb (1849-1930) see *DNB* and A.S. Gray, *Edwardian Architecture: A Biographical Dictionary*, 1985, pp.374-9. Webb's father-in-law, David Everett FRCS (d.1884) was a deacon of Angel Street Congregational Church, Worcester, 1858-80. W. Urwick, *Nonconformity in Worcester*, 1897, pp.127, 133

Huntingdon's Connexion.[10] You could be a cadet of the building baronage, so busy carving up Kensington and Belgravia, like Harold Peto, Howard Seth-Smith or W.F. and W.W. Pocock, whose origins were Baptist, Congregational and Wesleyan respectively.[11] Norman Shaw's favoured builder, John Grover, was a Finsbury Park and Stamford Hill Congregationalist who moved out to Hindhead and built there.[12] William Collins, who built much of Muswell Hill and whose sons atoned for their father's sins of commission by their own buildings in Southampton, was a Ferme Park Baptist.[13] James Edmondson, who built much of the rest of Muswell Hill and whose son became a Tory peer, was a Highbury Quadrant Congregationalist.[14] If you were creative, practical and intelligent, with little prospect of large inherited capital but with the safety net of the chapel connexion stretched to catch you, should you fall; disciplined by your upbringing and not yet cast into the classical grammar school mould; then architecture, like drapery, or the ministry, made sense. Dissent, in short, is a clue to context.

Where stand Norwich and Norfolk in this context? The Norwich of Old Meeting and Prince's Street for Congregationalists, St Mary's for Baptists, The Octagon for Unitarians, Calvert Street for Methodists or Goat Lane for

---

[10] For William Butterfield (1814-1900) see *DNB* and P. Thompson, *William Butterfield*, 1971

[11] For Harold Ainsworth Peto (1854-1933) see A.S. Gray *op.cit.*, p.284 and D.Ottewill, *The Edwardian Garden*, Yale University Press, 1989, pp.146-57. For William Howard Seth-Smith (1852-1928) see Gray *op.cit.*, p.324 and *The Builder*, 7 September 1928, p.394. For William Fuller Pocock (1779-1849) see *DNB*. For William Willmer Pocock (1813-99) see *The Builder* 30 September 1899 pp.308-9.

[12] For John Grover (d.1914) see C. Binfield, 'Hindhead Highmindedness', *PN Review*, 49, vol.12, no.5, 1986, pp.26-9

[13] For William Collins (1856-1939) and his family see R. Williams, *Herbert Collins 1885-1975: Architect and Worker for Peace*, Southampton, 1985

[14] For the involvement of the Edmondson family with Highbury Quadrant and Muswell Hill Congregational Churches see C. Binfield, 'Collective Sovereignty? Conscience in the Gathered Church c.1875-1918' in *The Church and Sovereignty c.590-1918*, ed. Diana Wood, Studies in Church History, Subsidia 9, Oxford, 1991, p.499; and C. Binfield, 'All Muswell Hill and Little Betty Martin: the establishing of a Congregational Church 1890-1925', *Victorian Values: Hornsey Historical Society Bulletin*, 31, 1990, pp.2-20

Quakers, needs little further celebration. What strikes the observer is the continuity across the denominations and down the generations of its opinion-forming nonconformity. This continuity has lasted from the seventeenth century to the twentieth and it has survived demographic and economic ebb and flow. There have been differing rhythms within it, now chiefly Unitarian or Quaker, now Baptist, now Congregational, but the continuity has been maintained. In the period which is our concern, it was maintained by the churches gathered in two chapels, Prince's Street Congregational and St Mary's Baptist. St Mary's, the 'fashionable watering place',[15] was the older but from the 1860s it was Prince's Street which set the pace. These two congregations sustained the causes of Old Dissent in the rest of Norfolk and they were nationally important in their respective denominations. Their ministers were Dissenting bishops. Their people were key strands, as the churches themselves were key points of intersection, in the familial webs of connexion which sustained the nonconformist interest.

In architectural terms Dissent both knew and enjoyed its place in this provincial capital. The Friends' Meeting in Goat Lane was unusually grand even for weighty Friends. The fascination which Thomas Ivory's Unitarian Octagon Chapel had for the visiting John Wesley is well-known.[16] Old Meeting expresses, with its touch of Dutch class, all that might be expected of mercantile Independency. The Baptists' fashionable watering place was certainly an elegant space. Only Prince's Street smacks conventionally of Chapel, punching the fact home in its overburdened street. It is with Edward Boardman (1833-1910), the man who stamped it thus, his son Edward Theobald Boardman (1861-1950), and some of their family connexions, that the rest of this paper is chiefly concerned, particularly Norman Jewson (1883-1975), whose brother married Edward's daughter, and Herbert Ibberson (1866-1935), who was Jewson's first cousin once removed. The Boardmans are representatively prolific of their type. Jewson is today the best regarded. Ibberson, who provides the core of the present study, also provides the most distinctively Dissenting insights.

---

[15] (Christopher Crayon), *Christopher Crayon's Recollections: the Life and Times of the Late James Ewing Ritchie*, 1898, p.13

[16] Wesley viewed it 23 December 1757. See, *inter alia*, J. Crouch, The *Planning* and *Designing of a Methodist Church*, Birmingham, 1930, pp.12-13

Edward Boardman was bedrock Prince's Street.[17] He was a deacon there. So were his brother, his father and his father-in-law, two sons-in-law, at least one second cousin and two second cousins-once-removed. J.J. Colman, the mustard manufacturer, was his second cousin by marriage as well as his son's father-in-law; and so one notes the point at which chapel bedrock becomes commercial bedrock. Since Edward the deacon became Edward the alderman one also notes the point at which chapel and commercial bedrock become civic bedrock.

Edward Boardman's family, therefore, was already upwardly mobile, making its way in business, educating its members sufficiently for their needs. Edward's brother James was, as has already been noted, a Prince's Street deacon.[18] His brother, Arthur, was for over fifty years local secretary to what is now Bishop's Stortford College, but was then still the 'East of England Nonconformist School'.[19] His brother Clement founded a dynasty of drapers. Clement's son, John Alexander (named after the minister who made Prince's Street the foremost chapel in Norwich), founded what became a department store in Stratford East. Consequently he lived in Woodford Green, that focus for East London's Free Church prosperity, and sent his sons to Mill Hill School. He gave them meaningful names: Howard Whittier, Wilberforce, Bruce. One of them became an estate agent, which brings us back to Edward's family.[20]

The marriages and futures of the daughters, Priscilla, Catherine, Edith and Ethel, and the sons, Ernest Charles and Edward Theobald, are part of our context.

Priscilla was Mrs Joseph de Carle Smith. The de Carles looked back to a seventeenth-century Norwich dyer whose descendants spread to Ipswich where they were Wesleyans, to Ely where they farmed and belonged to Lady Huntingdon's Connexion, or stayed in Norwich where they became Prince's

---

[17] Helen C. Colman, *Prince's Street Congregational Church, Norwich, 1819-1919*, 1919 *passim*

[18] *Ibid.*, p.75

[19] J. Morley and M. Monk-Jones, *Bishop Stortford College 1868-1968: A Centenary Chronicle*, 1969, p.49; *Congregational Year Book*, 1886, p.353

[20] E. Hampden-Cook, *The Register of Mill Hill School, London 1807-1926*, priv., 1926, pp.289, 301, 329, 374, 384

ARCHITECTURAL COUSINHOOD

Boardman / Jewson / Ibberson: An East Anglian and Dissenting Context for the profession of architecture

John THEOBALD = Mary Masters
1736-1799 — 1738-1780

- William 1767-1841
- Thomas 1774-1841 = Elizabeth Colman 1780-1859
- W.H. COZENS-HARDY 1806-1895 = Sarah 1808-1891
  - Herbert, 1st Baron
  - Sydney

Frances Newson = William 1767-1841
- Frances 1805-1874 = James BOARDMAN 1796-1839
  - Edward 1833-1910
  - Clement 1836-1923 (of Woodford & Stratford E)
  - James Theobald = Martha Brown 1836-1918
    - Edward 1861-1950 = Theobald
      - Humprey 1904-
    - Edith = W.W. Rix Spelman
    - Ernest 1869 = Ethel Gurteen
      - Catherine 1871-1958 = Daniel Gurteen 1872-1952
    - Priscilla = J. de Carle Smith
    - Ethel 1878-1966
    - Percy William M.P. 1881-1962
      - Charles Boardman 1909-1981
    - Mary = Norman 1883-1975
      - Edward 1900-

J.J. COLMAN M.P. 1830-98 = Caroline 1831-95
- Florence 1869-1950
- Laura 1859-1920 = James Stuart M.P.
  - Christopher
  - Stuart
  - Joan
- Russell 1861-1946
- Ethel 1863-1948
- Helen Caroline 1865-1947

George JEWSON of Earith 1794-1848 = Mary
- Charles = Mary IBBERSON
  - Herbert George IBBERSON 1866-1935
  - Kate Hewitt 1868-1934
- John Wilson 1816-1882 = Ellen Marshall 1827-1904
  - Charles = Harriet Caroline 1853-1866
    - Revd Frank Colin 1891-1972
    - Revd A. Keith 1899-
  - Revd Wyndham Colin BRYAN 1858-1919
  - George
  - Revd Arthur 1856-1931
    - John William 1851-1922
    - Sidney BARNSLEY 1865-1926
    - Ernest BARNSLEY 1863-1926
    - Campbell = Dorothy
      - Stephen (2) M.P.

Note

- IBBERSON — Congregational;Baptist (Hunstanton)
- JEWSON — Baptist (St. Mary's)
- BRYAN — Baptist
- BOARDMAN — Congregational (Princes Street, Woodford)
- THEOBALD — Baptist (St. Mary's, Old Meeting, Princes Street), Congregational
- COZENS-HARDY — Wesleyan, Free Methodist (Holt Free Methodists, Princes Street Congregational, Kensington)
- COLMAN — Baptist, Congregational (St. Mary's, Princes Street)
- BROWN — Congregational (Princes Street)
- STUART — Congregational, Presbyterian
- HEWITT — Congregational (Leicester)
- SPELMAN — Congregational (Princes Street)
- GURTEEN — Congregational (Haverhill)
- DE CARLE SMITH — Congregational (Princes Street)
- BARNSLEY — originally Wesleyan (Birmingham)

Street Congregationalists.[21] The de Carle Smiths began at St Mary's, where Priscilla's thrice-married grandfather-in-law was Sunday school superintendent and deacon. He became mayor of Norwich in 1877 and was the School Board's vice-chairman.[22] Joseph himself was a Prince's Street man, a connexion which survived into the 1980s.

Catherine was Mrs Daniel Gurteen. Like the de Carles the Gurteens claimed Flemish or Huguenot descent. They dominated Haverhill in the Independent belt which runs along the borders of Cambridgeshire, Essex and Suffolk. Indeed they 'were Haverhill'.[23] By 1885 the Gurteens' French Renaissance drabbet works employed 3,000 and covered four acres. Their great, red, spired Old Independent Church was as unlike an old Independent meeting as might be, though it was as up-to-date and internally artful as any London chapel. With their capacious houses (The Duddery, Chauntry, Coupals), and their long line of Daniels, the Gurteens were a dynasty. Catherine's Daniel was the fifth. Her grandfather-in-law, Daniel III, who was as long-lived as Priscilla's, was the empire builder. 'King of Haverhill', donor of its town hall and its chapel spire (120 feet, in memory of his wife), Daniel III was 'one of the finest captains of industry in East Anglia'. He chaired the School Board and the Gas Company. He directed the local railway and Bishop's Stortford College. Less expectedly he was Lord of a manor, patron of a living and farmed a thousand acres.[24] Daniel IV, who survived him a year, and Daniel V, Catherine Boardman's husband, continued this staunch tradition. Indeed, it continued, considerably attenuated, into the 1980s, justifying the claim made by the *Halstead Times* that 'Congregationalism had made the town of Haverhill what it was'.[25]

Edith was Mrs William Wilton Rix Spelman. Each of those names is

---

[21] I am indebted to Mr E. de C. Blomfield for information about the de Carles and de Carle Smiths

[22] For J. de Carle Smith (1812-1902) see C.B. Jewson *The Baptists in Norfolk*, 1957, p.105

[23] Sara Payne, *The Gurteens of Haverhill*, Cambridge, 1984

[24] *Christian World*, 9 June 1885

[25] *Halstead Times* 4 July 1885. The information about the Gurteens comes from a collection of cuttings belonging to Miss Grace Gurteen, who proved a mine of information about the Gurteens and their connexions

ARCHITECTURAL COUSINHOOD

imbued with 1662 Independency, chiefly Beccles, but also Bungay and Yarmouth. In Norwich the Spelmans had tended to be Old Meeting where, 'Up in the gallery were Spelmans and Jarrolds in abundance'.[26] The Wiltons, Rixs and Spelmans preached, brewed, farmed and auctioned. W.W.R. Spelman was an Old Millhillian, like the Woodford Boardmans. His family's firm of auctioneers and estate agents in Norwich and Yarmouth had begun in 1810.[27]

Ethel, the youngest of Edward Boardman's daughters, became Mrs Percy Jewson. The Jewsons were newcomers to Norwich and firmly St Mary's Baptists.[28] Their timber business had been established by Percy's father and uncle on their removal to Norwich from the Fens in 1868. By the middle decades of the following century it had taken sufficient root for Percy, one of those men who give teeth as well as clout and goodness to the causes of the voluntary sector, to become Lord Mayor of Norwich in the 1930s and its MP in the 1940s.[29]

So briefly, to the Boardman boys: Charles, who married a Gurteen, settled in Haverhill and became an estate agent like his cousin Wilberforce; and Edward Theobald, who became an architect like his father.

The scene is set: several generations of civic politics, philanthropy and nonconformity, soundly cushioned in business and usefully outposted in the world of building and property; an architect with an architect son and an estate agent and auctioneer great-nephew, and a timber merchant son-in-law.

III

Edward the alderman's professional formation was sound in clout and connexion. It began in Lowestoft in 1850 with the architect J.L. Clemence,

---

[26] Christopher Crayon, *op.cit.*, p.85

[27] Hampden-Cook, *op.cit.*, p.189; *Norfolk and Suffolk in East Anglia: Contemporary Biographies*, ed. E.C. Hopper, Brighton, 1911, p.342

[28] I am indebted to the late C.B. Jewson for much information about the Jewsons and their connexions

[29] For Percy William Jewson (1881-1962) see C.B. Jewson, *P.W. Jewson, Verses and a Biographical Note*, priv. Norwich, 1964; and M. Stenton and S. Lees, *Who's Who of British Members of Parliament*, vol.III, 1919-45, Brighton, 1979, pp.186-7

Lucas Brothers the builders and the world-embracing schemes of Morton Peto, the Baptist contracting impresario. All of them were young. Boardman was seventeen, Clemence and the Lucases were a dozen or so years older, even Morton Peto was only in his early forties. Peto had still to explode into the baronetcy and national fame with which the Crimean War endowed him, but he had already left building for the bigger world of railways and docklands and was now a man of affairs and philanthropies.[30] He had been MP for Norwich since 1847, which coincided suggestively with his development of Lowestoft's harbour, and squire of Somerleyton since 1846. His style was princely, his homes palatial and his reputation tempestuous. 'Many instances might be given of keen practice and prompt resource on the part of this well-known personage;'[31] and in 1847-8 he faced serious financial crisis. None of this seemed to dent his standing among Baptists. He was the century's first Baptist MP, and he had just built a Baptist cathedral in Bloomsbury, twin-spired and French Romanesque-fronted (the back was pure chapel), so that London could have an eligibly central Baptist preaching place. He put Norwich's William Brock in its pulpit.

The Lucas Brothers, Charles and Thomas, had served on Peto's staff.[32] Their careers shadowed his. They had taken over his building work and were in their turn to move into the heady world of public works contracting. Indeed Charles named his third son after Peto, and Thomas both took over Peto's town house and followed him into a baronetcy.[33] In the early 1850s, however, they had their Norfolk connexion to consolidate and Lowestoft to develop, as well as palazzi along Kensington Palace Gardens for the Petos to live in. John Louth Clemence, who outlived them all, was the one who stayed in Lowestoft, planning its esplanades and sitting on its improvement

---

[30] For Sir Samuel Morton Peto Bt. (1809-89) see *Biographical Dictionary of Modern British Radicals* eds J.D. Baylen and N.J. Gossman, vol.ii, 1830-70, Brighton, 1984, pp.407-11

[31] Thus the engineer (himself of Congregational origins) F.R. Conder in 1868: *The Men Who Built Railways: a Reprint of F.R. Conder's Personal Recollections of English Engineers*, ed. J. Simmons, 1983, p.101

[32] Charles Lucas (1820-95) and Sir Thomas Lucas Bt (1822-1902) - in 1852 Thomas Lucas married the daughter of a Norfolk notable, Robert Chamberlain of Catton. J. Summerson, *The London Building World of the Eighteen-Sixties*, 1973, pp.14-15

[33] Morton Peto Lucas, b. 1856

commission, captaining its volunteers and serving as mayor in 1886.³⁴ He worked for Peto and the Lucases, but as an architect rather than a builder or subcontractor.

In May 1855 Boardman completed his apprenticeship, received a gold hunter watch 'from LUCAS BROTHERS for his indefatigable perseverance and good conduct', and moved to superintend their work at Woolwich Arsenal.³⁵ By 1860, however, he was back in Norwich, married and in practice on his own account. His professional career was rock solid: the London Street Improvement Scheme (1876-80), the Norwich and Norfolk Hospital (1879-83), the Jenny Lind Infirmary and, as perhaps its culminating point, the conversion from 1886 of Norwich Castle from prison to museum. Boardman's commissions spread through the eastern counties: Gurney's Bank enlarged in Halesworth (1873); Peckover's Bank rebuilt in Wisbech (1878); almshouses in Barningham and a church school in Wingfield (1875); the Norfolk and Suffolk Yacht Club in Lowestoft (1886). It was all very up-to-date; the new building types; the professionalism (FRIBA 1871); the useful links; and the familial and denominational underpinning.³⁶

For Boardman's was still a chapel world, with work in brick and stone to prove it. He built in Norwich for the Ber Street Wesleyans (1868), the Unthank Road Baptists (1875) and the Theatre Street Presbyterians. He built especially for Congregationalists: chapel renovations and alterations at Harleston (1879), Bungay (1885-6), Beccles (1878-80) and Lowestoft (1881), the two last with new halls and classrooms. Two representative examples might be selected. The first, in three stages between 1868 and 1881, involved the virtual rebuilding of Prince's Street and the construction of a totally new block of lecture halls whose cost (£15,000) was more than that of most large chapels.³⁷ Prince's Street thumps its efficiency. It is a praying machine for active citizens. Cowper Memorial, East Dereham is quite another matter. It stands with its tower in the centre of the market town, gothic not

---

³⁴ For J.L. Clemence (1822-1911) see Cynthia Brown, B. Hazard and R. Kindred, *Dictionary of Architects of Suffolk Buildings 1800-1914*, Ipswich, 1991, p.75

³⁵ The watch remains with his descendants.

³⁶ For Edward Boardman (1833-1910) see *The Builder*, 26 November 1910, p.670; *Eastern Daily Press*, November 1910; E.C. Hopper, *op.cit.*, p.398; Brown, Haward and Kindred *op.cit.*, pp.48-9

³⁷ Helen C. Colman, *op.cit.*, p.51

Romanesque, a cause for polite farmers and drapers. East Dereham's vicar pondered it in his diary:

> Paid a visit to the new 'Congregational Church' in the market-place, on the site of the house in which the poet Cowper died. It indicates a wide departure from the previous ideas and traditions of the Independents. The interior is contrived to look as little like a conventicle as possible. The most curious thing of all is that the services, I am told, are not to be of the usual extempore character but are to consist of selections from the Book of Common Prayer, doubtless with the careful elimination of the well-known passages which have so long been a *crux* not only to Dissenters but also to their Puritan sympathizers in the Church of England. It certainly does credit to the liberality and taste of our Dissenters.[38]

Such changes in Dissenting ecclesiology reflected change in Dissenting society. From 1889 Boardman was in partnership with his son, Edward Theobald Boardman (1861-1950).[39] The younger Boardman was second generation in more ways than one. He went away to school, not indeed to one of the new nonconformist proprietary schools, like Bishop's Stortford, nor to one of the revived public schools, but to Amersham Hall. This was a remarkable private boys' school run first at Chenies and then near Reading by a Baptist father and son, Ebenezer and Alfred West. The school had Norfolk connexions. Several young Colmans and Cozen-Hardys were educated there. So were Morton Peto's two elder sons.[40] School over, Boardman was first articled to his father, then went as an improver to a London office. The choice was instructively sound: that of Ernest George.

---

[38] He added: 'The association of it with Cowper's name is more clever than justifiable, seeing that the poet lived and died in the Church of England. It has had a very misleading effect upon the minds of many, who have supposed that the building was consequently in connection and have thus unwittingly contributed to its erection'. Entry for 25 September 1874 *Armstrong's Norfolk Diary*, ed. H.B.J. Armstrong, 1963, p.140

[39] For E.T. Boardman see E.C. Hopper, *op.cit.*, p.285 and Brown, Haward and Kindred, *op.cit.*, pp.48-9

[40] Founded Chenies (1824), it moved to Amersham (1829) then Caversham (1861) and closed July 1892. Amersham Hall School, *Register of Open Scholarships, Fellowships, Honours and University Degrees, with Annotations and Summaries 1841-1886*, Reading, 1886; and *1841-1892*, Reading, 1892 (this is without the 'Annotations')

Ernest George, a wholesale iron merchant's son from south London, was already successful and increasingly fashionable.[41] He developed a line in great houses, commercial palaces and able pupils. Herbert Baker, Edwin Lutyens, Arnold Mitchell, R. Weir Schultz and E. Guy Dawber all passed through George's office as pupils or assistants. Dawber, who was Boardman's exact contemporary, was a fellow Norfolk man and became a lifelong friend.[42] It may be that he provided an opening for Boardman. More likely there had been some judicious drawing on the professional memory bank, for in 1875-6 George had taken Harold Peto into partnership.

Harold was Morton Peto's fifth son. Sir Morton was by now a shadow of his former self, but financial collapse had not submerged him and he could still pull strings. Harold, who was seven years E.T. Boardman's senior, was Harrow rather than Amersham Hall. But he had begun his professional career articled to Clemence of Lowestoft, and had then moved on to Lucas Brothers and to what remained of his family's empire in Peto Brothers. The moment he joined Ernest George, the partnership's prosperity bloomed. One of their first commissions was to alter Bloomsbury Chapel (1877), but their best remembered work is that apotheosis of *embourgeoisement*, the series of Renaissance extravaganzas built by Peto Brothers for the Cadogan Estates in Harrington and Collingham Gardens. Ernest George charmed clients by his watercolour perspectives, Harold Peto attracted clients by his useful connexions, both of them impressed clients with their concern for interior detail. Everybody benefited, especially Peto Brothers. Peto had another flair; he became a garden designer in the grand English manner, processional, classical and yet romantic.[43] The partnership's best-remembered pupils — Baker, Lutyens, Dawber, Schultz, Dan Gibson — were chief among the new architectural generation, whose houses were designed in close association with their pleasure grounds. E.T. Boardman's style was heavy and more prosaic, but this was his generation.

In 1898 Boardman married the sister of one of his school contemporaries. She was Florence Colman, his third cousin and the youngest daughter of J.J.

---

[41] For Sir Ernest George (1839-1922) see *DNB* and Gray, *op.cit.*, pp.186-7

[42] I am indebted to Mr H.C. Boardman for this information. For Sir E. Guy Dawber (1861-1938) see *DNB* and Gray, *op.cit.*, pp.160-3

[43] F. Whitsey 'A Style Writ Large', *Country Life*, 24 January 1991, pp.52-6; D. Ottewill, *op.cit.*, pp.146-58

Colman. That marriage can serve to focus our attention both on the continuities of the Boardman practice and on the domestic opportunities which increasingly presented themselves.

The staple work continued: board schools enlarged at Brandon in 1897; banks altered in Mildenhall (1893), Bury St Edmunds (1896) and Eye (1907); alterations for Halesworth's Congregationalists (1893). At the turn of the century there was a new church for the Congregationalists in Magdalen Road, Norwich, a ponderous essay in Romanesque red brick, stone dressed and flanked by two low dome-capped towers. It was an odd mixture of the mainstream, the efficient and the old-fashioned: mainstream and no-nonsense with its central rostrum and choir, organ to back, table in front; efficient with its electric lighting and its draught-excluding double-swing doors; old-fashioned with its iron-columned galleries. It was economical too, for it squeezed 850 sittings into a box no more than fifty-five by sixty feet, with kitchens, lavatories and schoolrooms in the basement and space for more at a later date.[44]

Magdalen Road was a new cause, only seven years old. It already had the third largest membership of Norwich's five Congregational churches, with 250 members to Prince's Street's 699 and 550 Sunday scholars to Prince's Street's 886.[45] It was built at the point when E.T. Boardman took over the practice. By then his father had been sixteen years a deacon at Prince's Street, thirteen years a town councillor and alderman for the last two. Five years later Edward Theobald himself was to become Mayor.

Houses were the practice's other staple. Large families and enlarged prosperity meant extensions to two Gurteen houses, Coupals and The Mount, both in Haverhill. For J.J. Colman there had been the Elizabethan transformation of The Clyffe, Corton, England's easternmost house which Colman had bought in 1869, and extensive work in Corton village, including the Free Methodist chapel (1873). Within Norwich there were steady improvements to Crown Point which Colman had purchased in 1872 and on which Edward Boardman had already worked in the late 1860s. When Russell Colman inherited the property the younger Boardman went to town on its conservatory wintergarden, a glazed fantasy in wrought and cast iron

---

[44] Estimated cost £6,000 *Congregational Year Book*, 1902, pp.146-7

[45] *Ibid.*, pp.302-3

and mosaic.⁴⁶

That was in 1902. Four years earlier he had begun to work for another brother-in-law, James Stuart, the Scotsman turned Cambridge academic turned Liberal politician turned starch and mustard man who had married Russell and Florence's eldest sister, Laura Colman, and had moved into Carrow Abbey.⁴⁷ With Carrow too there was a long Boardman connexion. Twenty years earlier Edward Boardman had advised J.J. Colman on the abbey's preservation. Now E.T. Boardman turned it into as much of an Edwardian country house as a dwelling so close to the shop could be, properly comfortable yet serious and civilised in deference to the property's past associations and present opulence. Stuart flattered himself that his new brother-in-law 'succeeded in doing this without in any way interfering with the historical part of it'.⁴⁸

Five years later Boardman was his own client. A favourite holiday stamping ground was Overstrand, where Boardmans had lived in the early eighteenth century and where Edward had a summer house. In 1903, however, Edward Theobald and Florence holidayed on the Broads and, coming in the pouring rain to a virtually treeless and totally isolated spot, they fell for it and bought it. There, at How Hill, Ludham, the E.T. Boardmans built and landscaped.⁴⁹ Building began in 1903. The house was white and thatched. Its design was reputedly influenced by buildings in India and Bavaria but this engaging eclecticism is undermined by more obvious references in its windows and chimneys. These are entirely vernacular, in an informed Edwardian Tudoresque, a touch Arts and Crafts, but with true Boardman heaviness. The grounds included formal and water gardens and involved great tree and hedge and flower plantings and imaginative landscaping. The estate ran to 360 acres. It formed a private nature reserve which remained Boardman property until 1966. The practice of architecture also remained with the family. In 1933 E.T. Boardman's second son, Humphrey Colman Boardman, joined the practice, which still continues.

---

⁴⁶ Jillian Powell, 'Last Chance for a Winter Garden', *Landscape*, January 1988, p.67

⁴⁷ For James Stuart (1843-1913) see J. Stuart, *Reminiscences*, priv., 1911

⁴⁸ *Ibid.*, p.268

⁴⁹ The story is told in a typescript, 'History of How Hill', 1980

IV

The Boardmans were a well-established Norwich family who had moved in from Overstrand. The Jewsons had moved much more recently into Norwich timber from Fenland farming. The Ibbersons were never Norwich though they became Norfolk. They too had farmed in the Fens, at Ramsey, moving into King's Lynn and Cambridge. Like the Jewsons, to whom they were several times related, they were Baptists. The Fen counties were Heinzlike in their Baptists, General, Particular, Strict, Johnsonian, with an admixture of Union Churches which combined Baptists and Congregationalists on equal terms as members, officeholders and pastors. This background is important for an understanding of Herbert Ibberson's attitudes.

Herbert George Ibberson (1866-1935) was of E.T. Boardman's generation and reared accordingly. He was educated not at Amersham Hall, but at Bishop's Stortford (1879-1882).[50] His professional training followed conventional paths — the Royal Academy Schools, overseas travel, a provincial practice and two London offices.[51] It was a sensible training in practicalities, lacking the main-chance implications of work, say, with Lucas Brothers but made humane by art, context and tradition. Like many of his architectural generation, Ibberson was a persuasive watercolourist. Such training and his travelling enlarged the cultural reservoir from which he drew his inspiration. His points of reference were from Italy and Germany as well as from the English countryside and his art was tactile as well as visual. Brick and flint and tile and fabric was where he excelled in colour and texture.

The offices in which he trained were sound, even seminal, for such development. The provincial office was that of Webb and Tubbs in Reading, with family connexion as the link. Cyril Bazett Tubbs's father was incumbent of St Mary's Castle Street, Reading. Cyril Tubbs's partner, George Webb, taught in its Sunday school.[52] St Mary's was an Anglican

---

[50] I am indebted to Mr W.E. Hall and Mr G.C. Gretham for confirmation of this

[51] This information is drawn from *The Builder*, 21 June 1935, p.1142 and RIBA Biographical Record

[52] I am indebted to Mr H. Godwin Arnold for information about C.B. Tubbs (fl. c. 1880-93) and G.W. Webb (b.1853)

proprietary chapel so four square in its Protestantism and so long associated with the elder Tubbs that it was known as 'Tubbs's Chapel' or simply 'Tubbs's'.[53] George Ibberson Tubbs, however, had not always been an Anglican. His background was Baptist, but he had been introduced to Norfolk Congregationalism at Burnham and trained in London Congregationalism at Highbury College before ministering to Wiltshire Congregationalism at Warminster. He had married, rather well as it turned out, into Manchester Congregationalism and his wife's Hopkinson and Wills kinsfolk (of engineering and Bristol tobacco note respectively) maintained amiable contact with the Tubbses.[54] An eligible Episcopalian proprietary chapel offered ample opportunity to a man whose Dissent was more Evangelical than political and such usefulness extended down the generations; hence the arrival in the 1880s of Herbert George Ibberson in the office of George Ibberson Tubbs's son.

C.B. Tubbs is a shadowy figure. His partnership with G.W. Webb was dissolved in 1886 and it is clear that Webb was the weightier partner. Some of Webb's training had been under E.W. Godwin[55] and this was reflected in a wide swathe of local work of no great distinction, but decently designed and competently handled in shades of Tudor, Dutch and medieval burgher. George Webb was a Tory and a Freemason and an antiquarian. He grew roses and chrysanthemums and had a 'thoroughly English fondness for athletic sports'. These characteristics colour his bluff Dick Whittington style and suggest why, politics and churchmanship notwithstanding, his was a foundational practice for young Ibberson.

The London offices in which Ibberson trained were ideal for fine-tuning a young Dick Whittington. John Belcher and John Dando Sedding were,

---

[53] G.I. Tubbs ministered at St Mary's Chapel 1852-88; it had begun as a preaching centre which was more Evangelical than Episcopalian and it spawned two Reading Congregational churches. Its overt Anglicanism was confirmed by its trustees in 1836: S. Yeo, *Religion and Voluntary Organisations in Crisis*, 1976, pp.142-3

[54] There are references to G.I. Tubbs in New College archives, Dr Williams's Library, 234/21 f 1-4; there are references to the Tubbses in Mary Hopkinson and Lady Ewing, *John and Alice Hopkinson 1824-1910*, nd., pp.XVI, XVII, 13, 15, 25, 48

[55] For E.W. Godwin (1833-86) see *DNB*

with Norman Shaw and Ernest George, the best London guides into the profession.⁵⁶ Belcher, who belonged to the Catholic Apostolic Church, is now most remembered for the 'Belcher' style (exemplified in the eastern counties by the riotous dignity of his baroque town hall in Colchester (1898-1902)). Sedding is best admired for his proposed Industrial Schools at Knowle, Bristol (1890) or his Holy Trinity, Sloane Street (1886-90). This was one of several churches to be a cathedral for that product of the 1880s, the Arts and Crafts Movement, and marks the stage at which the domestic revival slipped first into the fittings and then into the structure of church life and building. This is the world, literally next door but a generation down, of William Morris. It was mediated through Sedding to his chief assistant and eventual successor Henry Wilson and to Wilson's close friend E.S. Prior, and was celebrated in one of Sedding's best-regarded assistants, Ernest Gimson, who had entered Sedding's office on William Morris's advice in 1886.⁵⁷

What Ibberson gleaned from this may be deduced from a letter which he wrote to a nephew thirty years later:

> I've an open mind as to 'style' ... Gothic is fairly flexible and I rather lean to it, so long as you do not let the domanant [sic] past make you a copyist. The Renaissance is good too, so long as one isn't carried away under its influence to the pride of life. For quite little places 'Jordans' [the Quaker shrine], is a charming jumping off place. I'm personally fond too of the Italian Romanesque stuff, rather simple round arches, but with delicate late work in the fittings — but we must what ever we do steer between the rocks of pedantic copying and the whirlpool of striving to be 'original' — we must let practical requirements and the ideal of our worship dominate us — in the spirit which giveth life.⁵⁸

Sedding died in 1891. Henry Wilson took over the practice and Ibberson set

---

⁵⁶ For John Belcher (1841-1913), John Dando Sedding (1838-91) and Richard Norman Shaw (1831-1912) see *DNB*; see also Gray, *op.cit.*, for Belcher (pp.103-6), and Shaw (pp.325-9); and A. Saint, *Richard Norman Shaw*, 1976

⁵⁷ For Henry Wilson (1864-1934) see Gray, *op.cit.*, p.387; for E.S. Prior (1852-1932) see *ibid.*, pp.294-7; for Ernest Gimson (1864-1919) see *ibid.*, pp.193-5 and also Mary Comino, *Gimson and the Barnsleys*, 1980

⁵⁸ H.G. Ibberson to Revd F. Bryan, 13 August 1917: I am indebted to Revd A.K. Bryan for access to this

up on his own account. From 1892 his life was concentrated in two pleasant and healthy places (health was always a problem): Hampstead, and — following his marriage — Hunstanton. His practice was concentrated in three places: London (in Adelaide Place, St Martin's Lane and, from 1912, Lincoln's Inn), Cambridge and Hunstanton. At this point Belcher's office, Hampstead friendships, and Free Church affinities focused on Lincoln's Inn bring another architect into the picture. Thomas Phillips Figgis belonged to a widely spread clan of Evangelical Dubliners who tended when in England to be Congregationalists.[59] J.B. Figgis 'of Brighton' was a cousin; John Neville Figgis, the historian, theologian and Anglo-Catholic, was a second cousin.[60] Phillips Figgis had moved from a Dublin training to London's Royal Academy Schools and assistantships with A.E. Street and John Belcher, and finally his own office from 1886. He was a companionable, musical man (friends recalled his 'delightful baritone voice') who developed a usefully civilised London and Home Counties line in libraries and art schools, hospitals and tube stations. They flowed from Arts and Crafts through Art Nouveau into Wrenaissance in a businesslike sort of way while he 'practised his profession in Lincoln's Inn, three or four friends joining him although not in partnership'.[61] One of those friends was Herbert Ibberson.

There were all sorts of links. In 1890 the Ladbroke Grove Free Library competition had been won by Figgis, working with Henry Wilson from Sedding's office. He became the Presbyterian Church of England's architectural adviser and designed churches for it at Ealing, Golders Green and Oxford (the last with a decently panelled, college hallish interior). He married a daughter of J.B. Paton, most educationally creative of Victorian Congregational ministers,[62] and designed the Home for Epileptics which Paton founded at Lingfield. Although Figgis sang at one time in the choir of St Mary Abbots, he is nonetheless remembered as more of a Congregationalist. When the family moved down to Beckenham Mrs Phillips

---

[59] For Thomas Phillips Figgis (1858-1948) see Gray, *op.cit.*, p.179

[60] John Benjamin Figgis (1837-1916) was the notable minister of Brighton's Countess of Huntingdon's Connexion Church; for his son, John Neville Figgis (1866-1919) see *DNB*

[61] So recalled William A. Pite, *RIBA Journal*, 1948, p.374

[62] For John Brown Paton (1830-1911) see *DNB*

Figgis joined the Penge Congregational Church, while two Figgis sisters, moving up to Hampstead, had married brothers who were early activists in another of suburban London's characteristically surprising chapel communities, the Lyndhurst Road Congregational Church.[63] That was in the 1890s, when Herbert Ibberson was living on Parliament Hill Road and joining in its manifold activities.

'This Church stands aggressively at the foot of the last ascent from London to Hampstead', whose 'inhospitable gradients' were falling swiftly to the building trade. Thus H.H. Asquith, who as a young barrister had been in on the church's beginning and now found it, twenty-one years later, 'a not unfitting symbol and expression' of the new life of Hampstead today'.[64] The cause was thus still new and it was still growing, an electric fusion of upwardly mobile professional families, refugees from Clapton or Islington, City folk in ample retirement and young men and women in training for nursing or medicine or education or the ministry or commerce or the law. It was hothouse and seed bed, a church for the professionally Dissenting professional classes in which Greek could meet Hebrew as in prophecy the lion would lie with the lamb. And it had building and minister to match.

The building was a Waterhouse Octagon in mauve brick. Ibberson approved of it. He found it 'good and, for a wonder, [its] great vault, like a dome, has no echo'.[65] Its minister, R.F. Horton, eleven years Ibberson's senior, was a Shrewsbury educated classic who had been president of the Oxford Union and then the first Fellow of an Oxford College to have simultaneous charge of a Congregational church since Cromwell's day. For fifty years Horton gathered that church's devotion; and he was never

---

[63] For information about T.P. Figgis, I am indebted to Dr Morton Figgis, Mr Nigel Figgis, Mr A.A. Smith and the Revd J.H. Taylor who confirms that Mrs T.P. Figgis joined Penge Congregational Church 6 November 1921. Her brother, John Lewis Paton (1863-1946: see *DNB*), later a famous High Master of Manchester Grammar School, was a member of Lyndhurst Road from 1899: *Lyndhurst Road News Sheet*, July 1899, p.2

[64] Asquith's hearers also included S. Figgis (1861-1920) uncle of J.N. Figgis and cousin of T.P. Figgis. The church's membership in 1901 was 1200 [Lyndhurst Road Congregational Church] *Thanksgiving Celebration October 1901*, p.5

[65] H.G. Ibberson to Revd F.C. Bryan, 13 August 1917

ordained.[66]

This was the place for men like Ibberson; his particular place in it was the Young Men's Guild which flickered and flourished between 1892 and 1898.[67] Ibberson was its secretary for a while (1892-4) and a contributor to its gaiety of spirit throughout. It met fortnightly on Tuesdays at eight to debate in members' homes the principles of Henry George or to hear Basil Martin, Horton's assistant,[68] on 'Robert Owen: the first English socialist'. They spoke impromptu one February Tuesday on leading articles from the morning's *Daily Telegraph*, and met the next Tuesday fortnight to discuss William Morris's *News from Nowhere* and Edward Bellamy's *Looking Backward*. It was precious, of course: 'The ordinary meetings of the Society have not been well attended, but have had an interest of their own peculiar to small meetings'. It was also beyond price: the June day when they rowed from Reading to Maidenhead; the evening of music with the Mosers of Maresfield Gardens; the British Empire with the Jamiesons in Hampstead Hill Gardens; Carlyle at Frognal, Browning in Gainsborough Gardens, Shakespeare in Fitzjohn's Avenue and Boswell's *Johnson* at Haverstock Hill's Ivybank with the Ridley Baxs. Bertie Ibberson's part in this was loyally suggestive: a discussion to be led on women's rights in 1892 (his Jewson kinswomen included pioneer professionals in medicine, politics and education); Free Trade, the country's salvation, to be debated in 1895 (he opposed it); the Architecture Around Us (in Belsize Square) in 1893; a paper on Browning and another on 'English Cathedrals, their Architecture and State of Preservation' in 1896; and, for perspective's sake, 'An amusing poem ... setting forth, in the well known metre of Longfellow's 'Hiawatha' a mistake of the Secretary in postponing a meeting of the Society, and at the last moment being compelled to revoke the order and call together a meeting at an hour's notice'. It was 'one of the most original efforts of the evening'.

This was more than mutual endeavour, for here were young professional men in their twenties and thirties transposing their skills into their leisure.

---

[66] For Robert Forman Horton (1855-1934) see *DNB*. He married a niece of T.P. Figgis in 1918

[67] The details of what follows came from a bound volume of the *Lyndhurst Road News Sheet*, November 1887 to January 1902, in the writer's possession

[68] Father of Kingsley Martin (1897-1969) later Editor of the *New Statesman* for whom see *DNB*

Thomas Horder was one, on his rapid way to 141 Harley Street.⁶⁹ Ibberson was another, already ARIBA (1889), soon enough to be FRIBA (1900), exhibiting at the Royal Academy by 1898,⁷⁰ displaying in the Young Men's Guild's sympathetic surroundings his SPAB concern for preservation and his Arts and Crafts concern for vernacular beauty and rightness (as in 'The Architecture Around Us') and setting the whole in Lyndhurst Road's frame of a still dissident citizenship.

So it was when he moved to Hunstanton. There his church was Union Church, a cause for holidaying Baptists and Congregationalists which had been the Ibberson family church since its stonelaying in July 1870. Herbert's involvement was confirmed by marriage. Herbert Ibberson's background was Baptist. Kate Ibberson's was Congregational. The Hewitts had moved from Northamptonshire to Leicester when Kate's father, Francis Hewitt (1832-97), became a printer's apprentice on the *Leicester Mercury* before setting up as a newsagent and bookseller. He did so well that in 1877 he bought the *Mercury* and became mayor of Leicester in 1883. He was also a founder of Leicester's Clarendon Park Congregational Church, that civic essence of congregational pride and architectural good sense; and from the 1890s he had a house in Hunstanton.⁷¹

Herbert Ibberson's own service to church and community in Hunstanton meant the committee of the local RSPCA, the treasurership of the local Red Cross, the chairmanship of the 'Advancement Association'. It meant advice on a bandstand for the Esplanade, on festivities for King George's Coronation, on the preservation of St Edmund's Chapel. When war came he addressed the local Volunteer Corps and busied himself with the enlisting of

---

⁶⁹ For Thomas, 1st Baron Horder (1871-1955) see *DNB*

⁷⁰ *The Builder*, 21 June 1935, p.1142; RIBA Biographical Record

⁷¹ *The Leicester Mercury*, a Liberal newspaper until 1924 was controlled by three generations of Francis Hewitts until 1954. I am indebted to the *Leicester Mercury* for information and to Mrs D.B.L. Hoegger for confirmation of the Hewitts's involvement with the Clarendon Park Church. See also *Leicester Mercury*, 31 January 1974 and for Francis Hewitt (1832-97) see H. Hartopp, *Roll of the Mayors of the Borough and Lord Mayors of the City of Leicester 1209-1935*, Leicester, 1936, pp.217-8

able-bodied men 'willing to help their country in this National Crisis'.[72]

This, with his health, is the context for Ibberson's architecture: mainly domestic, but with some commercial, scholastic, restorative and ecclesiastical commissions. Ibberson houses were the sort to have names — Markinch, Carstone, Burlington Cottage, The Gables — and his Hunstanton houses stand out along Lincoln and Boston Squares, Northgate and Austin Street, not too large, scaled for the seaside but better than boarding houses. The Gables, his own house, has more than a touch of Hampstead-by-the-Sea, but they are pleasantly eclectic houses of the late Arts and Crafts, styled in country baroque, but quite incapable of restraining the sort of Art Nouveau nonsense that the seaside brings out in respectable citizens. They show a liking for heavy mullions, flint chequer patterning, russet red brick and russet brown stone. In them Edgar Wood's Yorkobethan or Ernest Gimson's Cotswold were translated to Norfolk with more than a touch of whatever was modish in the air. Mackintosh, Voysey, Baillie Scott, Francis Troup lurk in the door furniture, in lead sundials on side walls, in oak settles elongated by fantasy and wood friezes fretted with the cloverleaf trefoil. These are not the borrowings of a country practitioner so much as the translations of a man who had trained at the heart of it all, their colloquialisms and clichés as well as subtler idioms permeating all his work. For all Ibberson's buildings were on a domestic scale, although his ecclesiastical work is pivotal to an understanding of this, with Hunstanton's Union Church pivotal to that.

Externally Union betrays little beyond the straitened respectability of inexpensive Gothic. Its stonelaying in 1870 was by a provincial commercial prince (sensibly and naturally he was J.J. Colman) and its opening in 1871 was by a metropolitan pulpit prince. Until 1889 it was little more than a preaching station. Then a minister was called and in 1890 a church was formed.[73]

From 1893 to 1899 Union's minister was a Baptist whose family now enters this story at several points: Wyndham Colin Bryan, a Cotswold

---

[72] His brother-in-law, Arthur Leicester Hewitt (1883-1950) of Northgate, Hunstanton, was a pioneer motorist, a military correspondent for *The Times* and creator of 'one of the best and most modern model armies in the world'. *Leicester Mercury*, 14 June 1950. I am indebted to Mrs K. Hooper, Mr W. Heap and the Revd Canon W.M. Jacob for much information about Ibberson in Hunstanton

[73] R.G. Martin, *These Hundred Years: A Picture of Union Church, Hunstanton 1870-1970*, Hunstanton, 1970, p.2

farmer's son who had trained at Spurgeon's Pastors' College.[74] To the evangelicalism presupposed by such a formation should be added a lively concern for worship's setting. The two were fused in a spirituality which Bryan sustained in four small pastorates: Bluntisham, Hunstanton, Rickmansworth and Ampthill. At Bluntisham he married Caroline Jewson who, though she now lived in Norwich, had been born like all her generation of Jewsons at Earith, not far from Bluntisham. Caroline Bryan was Bertie Ibberson's first cousin and as was frequently the way in large families these links intensified when Bertie's brother Charles married Caroline's sister Harriet and again when Caroline's brother Herbert and Bertie himself both married half-sisters. Bryan and Ibberson had much in common. There were only eight years between them. Both enjoyed poor health. It is hard not to see Ibberson influence behind Bryan's move from Bluntisham to Hunstanton in 1893. There, as at his two subsequent pastorates, Bryan stamped his personality physically on the cause. On each occasion his agent was Herbert Ibberson.

Union was very much the Ibberson church. The 'imaginative genius of members of the Ibberson family ... has given to the Chapel the dignity which belongs to the ensemble of pulpit, choirstalls and panelling'. Thus the chapel history.[75] The organ was built in 1900 in memory of Herbert's father, Charles Ibberson of Lynn and Cambridge, who had been one of Union's founders, and it was restored in 1935 in memory of Herbert's wife, Kate Mary. The communion chairs were in memory of Herbert Ibberson. And the style throughout, from W.C. Bryan's promptings onwards, was his.

The three communion chairs are the most distinctive furnishings. They are Arts and Crafts of purest essence, the ultimate in stripped Queen Anne. It is in the tendrilled windows that Art Nouveau breaks out, their stylised design of what might be a standard rose, or a long-stemmed lily, forming perhaps a cross or suggesting rather a three-branched candlestick, their trinity fusing in flame: lily, rose, cross, trinity, pentecost- or simply coloured glass on which wandering attention might linger? There is more: the roof trusses with their fretted heart motif; the pine communion table with its heart motif

---

[74] I am indebted to Revd A.K. Bryan for information about W.C. Bryan (1858-1919); and to W. Heap, 'The Free Church (Baptist) Hillside Road, Chorleywood and a History of its Architecture', Open University B.A. Dissertation, 1976, p.2

[75] Martin, *op.cit.*, p.7

too; the small repoussé copper plaques, one with a sun, expressing religions which worship God in nature, one with a square and a heart and a circle, emblems of honesty, charity and wholeness, for those religious people who, though ignorant of God in Jesus, yet seek to live uprightly, and one, supreme, as the cross-bearing Lamb of God.[76] Throughout, the symbolism, though reticent, is insistent:

> Each hymn board ... proclaims a truth about hymn-singing. At the top of the board on the left of the congregation there is carved an ill-nourished bird; one of its legs is broken, and its wings hang helplessly down; it is surrounded by dying leaves and rose petals and above is the cross of suffering. Yet the bird still sings, and across the face of the board are the Latin words — *Dolens Lauda*: when in sorrow, praises. There are arrows among the leaves, but they are only reminiscent of St Edmund, the patron saint of Hunstanton.
> The bird at the top of the other hymn board is well-favoured and uninjured; roses and rose-leaves in full beauty are surmounted by a crown of triumph and the bird is in full song: *Gaudens Lauda* is the message — when rejoicing, praises.[77]

Here, mellowing and colouring and catholicising (or, rather, universalising) the starved Gothic, are joined the religious nonconformity of Spurgeon and of Horton, of Hampstead and the Elephant and Castle, Matthew Arnold truly turned Salvation Army Captain on the North Norfolk coast, an art to agonize as well as charm for a church which could oppose the Boer War and encourage Passive Resistance as well as minister to resident trippers.

In 1899 Bryan moved on to his longest pastorate, Rickmansworth. This too was a happy, lively and growing product of leisured consumerism. And it included Chorleywood. That spot was ideal. With wooded hills and valleys for privacy and variety, the railway (1889) for helpful access and C.F.A. Voysey at The Orchard on Shire Lane (from 1899), Chorleywood was a Chiltern paradise for sensitive developers who could see profit in Arts and Crafts. What John Grover of Stamford Hill was doing for Hindhead, his fellow builder (and Dissenter), James Beckley of Watford, did for Chorleywood. Beckley offered Bryan a site and £200 for a chapel. It was to be at the corner of South and Hillside Roads, settling as their names implied south-

---

[76] *Ibid.*, p.10

[77] *Ibid.*, p.9. The wording, though unattributed, bears all the hallmarks of Ibberson's style.

facing into the wooded hill on whose crest lived Voysey. Bryan approached his Hunstanton cousin-and-brother-in-law, H.G. Ibberson. From this convergence of pious speculation, evangelical determination and artistic specialism issued a scheme which was at once visionary and cautious.[78]

The vision was exhibited at the Royal Academy in 1906: a water colour perspective of a great church, a Baptist Holy Trinity, Sloane Street or St Peter's, Mount Park, Ealing, to gladden the heart of a Sedding or Henry Wilson, a monumentally vernacular communion of all those elements — Gothic and Renaissance and Italian Romanesque — which Ibberson most favoured in church architecture. Such was the vision. The caution was apparent a year earlier in the *Builder's Journal* account of the first stage which most chapel speculations went through: 'The building committee readily agreed to allow the chapel to be very simple in character, and desired to make no attempt with the thousand pounds at their disposal to imitate the glories of a parish church'.[79]

It may be felt, however, that what was actually done was more interesting as well as more Baptist. It met the urgency of need. There must be a rapid start and there was £1,197 in hand. The result was a church built in five months which might one day turn into a hall; that is to say, there resulted a meeting-house, at once public and domestic, whose allure must depend on line, texture and sympathetic colour. Hence the long, low, yellow stockbrick walling, the gentle arches, the roughcast in the gables, the Monk Park stone for the golden-brown mullions and the grey green slates for the low sweeping roof. Hence, too, the architect's trademarks, Arts and Crafts stylised here (as at Hunstanton) into an Art Nouveau: repoussé lead panels on the turret, symbols of the Crucifixion; repoussé lead over the entrance, vine leaves and 'I am the Door' in Greek and 'My House shall be called the House of Prayer' carved over the porch; plain oak doors; ventilator openings with red burnt clay tiles fitted into them; buttresses with chequered brick and flint, all so gently contrived that the intensity of such contriving is barely apparent.

Inside, it was just a large, white-ceilinged hall, its contrivances only there if looked for — in the rush-seated chairs; in the red-brown, herring-bone pine floor; at the end wall, arched to frame the platform with the arch pale yellow and its gable pale blue flanked in white; behind the country oak table in the

---

[78] The following account is drawn chiefly from Heap, *op.cit.*

[79] *The Builder's Journal*, 3 May 1905, p.238

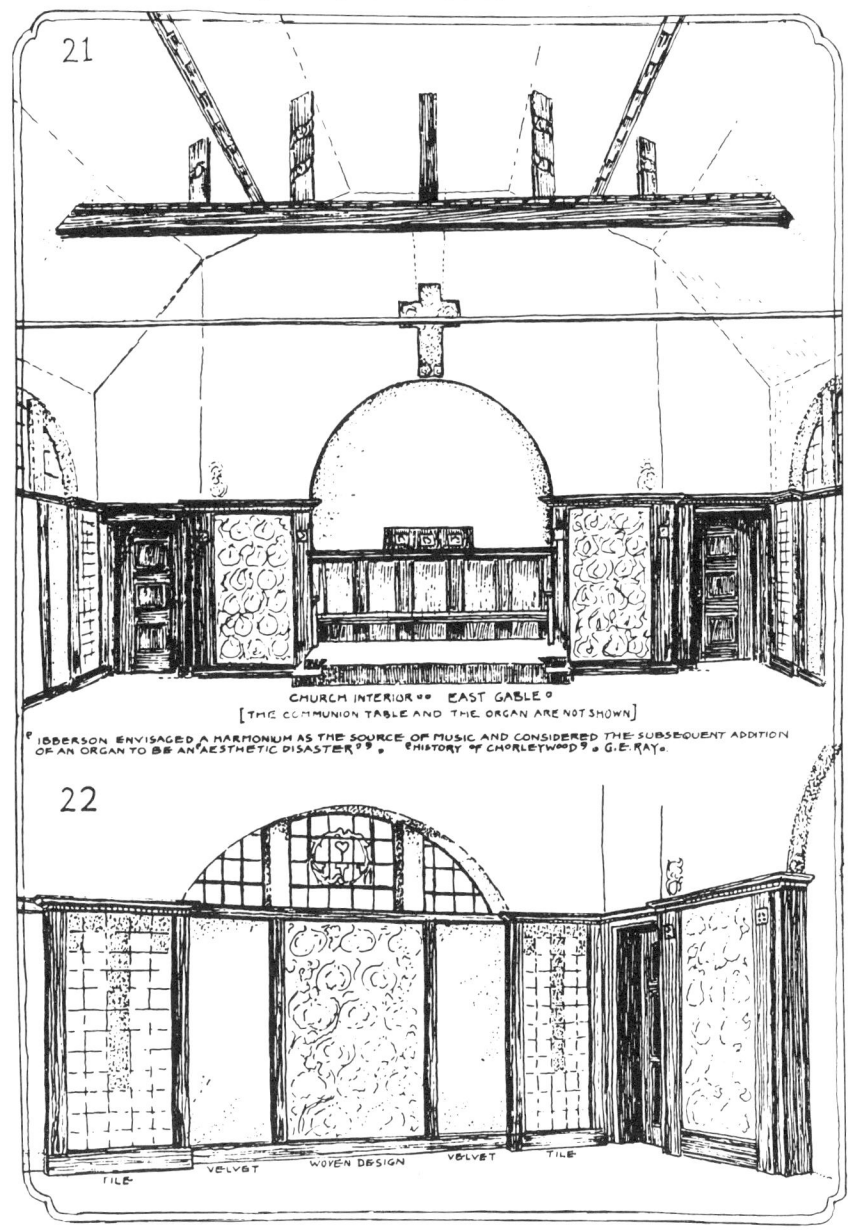

Chorleywood Free Church: interior, 1905. This was the first stage in a scheme to build a much grander church. The interior is a surprising Baptist tribute to Voysey-accented Arts and Crafts.

panelled bench whose back supported the lectern and formed the pulpit's front. There is contrivance in the windows near the east end with their design of a heart, a crown of thorns, three nails, in blues and greens which accentuate the glass's liquid quality. At the west end the window was round, enclosing three crosses in frosted glass, with a blue-green Calvary stylised in the segment above. There was contrivance in the dado along the wall — panels of tapestry, velvet and faience framed in dark-stained pine flank the platform, with more faience panels, deep blue with 'T' motifs in dark green set between the windows. So the contriving continued — in the west doors below the Calvary windows, for example, flanked and matched by cupboards and topped by repoussé copper plaques with a cross design. The Cross is the chief contrivance, most evangelical where least expected, for a repoussé cross in hand-made copper hangs from the white ceiling, carefully lit from behind.

Chorleywood's Baptist meeting-house has naturally led observers to ponder the debt to Voysey, just up the hill at The Orchard. This may never be directly proved. One may merely note the Voyseyan touches, the grey-green slates and overhanging eaves, the piano stool with its heart ('commercialised Voysey'), the communion chairs, ('part Voysey, part country'), the mortar-board tops to the woodwork, the vestry fireplace so like one in an Orchard bedroom, the tapestry panels from a Liberty design, the dado's japonaiserie of dark wood frame against white walls.[80]

Although the big church was never built, this was not the end of it as far as Ibberson was concerned. In 1934 Charles Brown, recently retired from an almost legendary north London pastorate at Ferme Park, was given £35,000.[81] Brown decided to spend this anonymous largesse on halls for Chorleywood's Baptists in memory of his wife. Once more Ibberson (whose own wife died in 1934) was called in and in sixty-three days the Florence Brown Memorial Hall was built: the stone laid 29 September, the hall opened 1 December. This, too, is in yellow brick with greenish slates and red tile, though the sweeping roof here becomes a mansard, echoing some of Ibberson's Hunstanton houses and allowing literally for domesticity since the scheme included a caretaker's house. Here texture is all, for Art Nouveau has faded away leaving art to the deeply arched porch, welcoming one, drawing the visitor inside.

---

[80] This is the main theme of Heap, *op.cit.*, esp. pp.13-16

[81] For Charles Brown (1855-1947) see *Baptist Hand Book* 1948, p.272

Ibberson worked for Roman Catholics and Anglicans as well as Free Churchmen,[82] but two Free Church commissions from the end of his life, this time for Congregationalists, merit consideration. One of them shows the now old-fashioned, sensitive conservationist, the other the creative artist.

Elmers End in 1930 was the sort of neighbourhood which later estate agents would call 'bright' or 'popular'. In the past five years its population had grown from five to ten thousand: 'New houses and new streets have sprung up, a new school, shops and factories are being built'.[83] It was prime housing estate country, close to fields as well as to Beckenham. Village Congregationalism had been there since 1884 and a church since 1902. By 1930 the village style had given way to a Sunday school of 200, a church of ninety-seven and a minister with a science degree and pacifist convictions.[84] The village was now a mission field:

> Except for an 'Anglo-Catholic' Church, and an 'Old Baptist', the Congregational Church is facing the real needs of this growing township.
> By an arrangement with the other Free Churches, it has been agreed that Congregationalists must provide for the Free Church people in this district. It is already in fact and practice a Union Church.

So the existing site on Goddard Road was enlarged and an architect introduced by London's Congregational Union and an appeal issued: 'This little boat is already loaded to the gunwale, and we send out this signal to "the other ships"'.

Ibberson was the architect, and his appeal echoes forty years on the young professional man who had debated and impromptued at Lyndhurst Road's Young Men's Society, painting in words as persuasive a watercolour as any of his mentors and displaying in his advocacy a sure knowledge of Free Church weaknesses and a skilfully impassioned understanding of Free

---

[82] He worked on Hunstanton's Roman Catholic Church and the baptistry and vestry of St Edmund's, Hunstanton and added a wing to its vicarage; he transformed a small Congregational church at Beer in Devon

[83] Elmers End Congregational Church, *Appeal Brochure*, on which this account is based.

[84] A.G. Knott (1889-1976) ministered at Elmers End 1923-32. Reared a Baptist, a Millhillian who played lacrosse for England and listed drama, mountaineering and social reform as his interests. E. Hampden-Cook, *op.cit.*, p.268; *United Reformed Church Year Book*, 1977, p.268

Church needs. It is a rich demonstration of Art and Craft and it shows how chapel building worked:

> My duty was (a) to try to design a building suitable for its purpose, and (b) to carry out the instruction of the Committee. I do not intend to imply that these things are antithetical.
>
> A suitable church is one in which people can speak, hear and see well, be comfortable — and so far as things material can help — be attuned to appreciate things spiritual.
>
> At Elmers End I am sure people can see — the church is light, and there are no pillars in the way — and I think they can speak, sing and hear well. But I am sure they won't all be comfortable. Comfort depends on heating and ventilation, and on the question of warmth and density of air men differ as they do on the less important matters of theology. One has on the one side the fresh (and sometimes cold) air modernist, and on the other the conservative fundamentalist who holds that cosiness becomes the courts of the Lord.
>
> I make a suggestion of a course of conduct which may in part remove a cause of offence to both right and left. *Have all the windows opened immediately after every service ends* and shut (more or less) before the next begins.
>
> I, with some impertinence stress this point, open the windows immediately the minister has left the pulpit, let the winds of heaven rush through and so avoid the feeling of froustiness which is I am afraid associated in the minds of the ungodly with organized religion.
>
> An unusual instruction from the Committee was conveyed to me through Mr Knott [the minister]. He said 'We have but little money, but should there be any to spare beyond producing the barest needs — spend it on a little extra height rather than on applied ornament'. I have done so, and the building is almost violent in its stark austerity.
>
> Yet I have tried to make it cheerful, even gay, and while I hope that conversation may be hushed and thoughts weaned from the irrevalences [sic] which beset us all, I hope no troubled soul will be depressed by its surroundings, but be sent away to face the world with greater courage and a quieter mind.
>
> I hope no one will be offended by the central and honourable position of the communion table, under its canopy of blue and gold. I understand that a time of silence is a part of the service at Elmer's End, and in silence (unlike in sermon time), one's mind is apt to wander. Will not the 'holy table' reminding us of our Lord's life and death and abiding presence, help more to devoutness than the most resplendent organ pipes? And then on 'Communion

Sunday', let the table be brought down from its high place, cover the cloth of gold with plain linen, gather around it as a family in simple fellowship and remembrance, and so by the very change of position emphasize our Protestant Faith.

I hope none will be offended at the little Latin on the 'tester'. I know Latin has a sinister suggestion, calling up obscurantism and cruel things. But it's a fine sonorous tongue, it's dead, so it can never die or be corrupted, even by America. And it is the only universal tongue. If a Briton [sic] peasant peddling onions looks through an open door, he will understand — and the Italian organ-grinder, or the Bavarian cornet-player in a German band, and the public school boy from — anywhere. All will know what 'Jesus Hominum Salvator' means. And it will link all together, Quaker, Catholic, Baptist, Independent, Unitarian. Jesus is the Saviour of Men to them all, though as to *how* they are saved they may all differ, and perhaps none understand.

Outside, the gable stands up high among the friendly little houses. I would have further emphasized it by a flèche on the ridge, had there be [sic] any money forthcoming. Bunyan and Milton guard the Free Church (Congregational) principles. The symbol of the Church invisible stands in the great window, a Cross, valiant and made joyous with gold for 'He is risen'.

Under the arch of the entrance is carved 'Come unto me all ye that Labour'. I expect that 'labour' will be held to mean suffering as well as work. I am sure that the poor will always be welcome, and I trust that even the rich will not be sent empty away.[85]

Timeless, and of its time; this placing in the Catholic church of a free church whose 'very beauty and severity give just what is often lacking in Nonconformity, a subtle appeal to the subconscious'; this freedom with symbol; this whimsical, affectionate intimacy with mystery; this home for an extended family; this banqueting hall with its high seat for the king, guarded without by Puritans in Ham Hill stone and within by angels holding

---

[85] When this appeal was printed in the neighbouring Beckenham Congregational Church's monthly magazine 'A Subscriber' wrote in:
> I notice that the architect ... apologises for the use of a Latin quotation, and says that Latin, being a dead language, can never be 'corrupted even by America'. This is very good news, but I must confess to receiving a severe shock when I saw that in the quotation over the entrance to the Church the word 'labour' was Americanized and spelt 'labor'.
> Will Mr Ibberson replace the American word by the English?

'A Query', *The Outlook*, March 1931, vol.2, 1931, no.15, p.91

bowls of electric light up to the barrel vault of rough yellow plaster. Austere? Yes, with the black pulpit and organ case. Reformed? Certainly, a high, Calvinist space, its table to be covered in white without fringe or lace, 'to emphasize the fact that the people break bread as brethren to remember the death of their Lord, rather than stand afar off while the sacrifice is enacted by a priest'.[86] Catholic? Of course.

Like Chorleywood, Elmers End was never completed. The intention was to extend it with a chancel and to broaden it with a parlour and vestries. That never happened. War intervened, damaging the great west window. The 'fall of sky blue damask of great height' has long since been replaced by a plain wooden cross, but the ten angels still throw electric light from their golden bowls.

The interior was stripped vernacular rather as contemporary cinemas might be stripped classical, but it led directly to a commission of pure nostalgia.

Elmers End's godparents were the Congregational churches in Crescent Road, Beckenham and Beckenham Road, Penge. Penge Congregational Church was the creation of 'Barson of Penge', Ernest Barson, for whom Percy Morley Horder in 1912 produced a great grey Free Gothic banqueting hall, fit for some grand Christian guild.[87] Morley Horder, himself a son of the manse, was a precocious practitioner, slightly Ibberson's junior, who excelled where Ibberson excelled, but with more panache and worldly success. By 1931 Horder had left his formative Congregationalism and was picturesquely *en route* for the Rome of the Chesterbellocians. He was also becoming impossible to work with. Consequently when the Penge Congregationalists wanted to incorporate a memorial chapel within Horder's fine space Barson turned to Herbert Ibberson whom he was encountering at Elmers End, and of whom he perhaps already knew through Phillips Figgis. The chapel was to commemorate a Bermondsey metal-box manufacturer, Alfred Feaver, who had been Penge's treasurer since 1908. Feaver had died in 1931 and his memorial, to be opened in April 1933, twenty-one years after the building's opening and twenty-five years after the church's formation,

---

[86] *CYB*, 1931, p.211

[87] For Ernest Barson (1877-1956), minister 1909-47, see *CYB*, 1957, p.510; for P.R. Morley-Horder (1870-1944) see *DNB*. His father was a cousin (and patient) of Thomas Horder, the physician, and Lyndhurst Road Member in the 1890s

Elmers End Congregational Church: elevation. In Ibberson's words, 'the building is almost violent in its stark austerity ... high among the friendly little houses.'

was to be a Chapel of Youth.[88]

Ibberson created his chapel by enclosing the church's north transept with an oak screen. Youth was celebrated by two paintings behind the chapel's communion table. These were copies of paintings planned for Sarum Chase, the new Hampstead home of Frank Salisbury, the Free Churchman who between the Wars was the British establishment's deftest portrait painter, a Thomas Lawrence for his time.[89] Salisbury was too busy to paint the pictures himself so his assistant Reginald Lewis painted them in Salisbury's studio leaving the master, so it is believed, to add the finishing touches. Certainly Salisbury was at Penge for the unveiling, so that he could expound their meaning. At Penge, as at Caius, Cambridge, you enter through the gate of Honour, although when you leave the same gate has become Humility, your transition helped by Salisbury's paintings and Ibberson's art. One of the pictures, *The Human Awakening*, depicts a youth armed for conflict in front of the archway of his past life, the arch of parents and home and school and church. The other, *Duty's Call*, shows him surrounded by an angel with a trumpet. 'When he answers that call, he will receive the helmet which rests in the crook of the angel's arm.'[90]

So here as at Hunstanton, this time in the decade of the Oxford Union's debate on King and Country, we have more echoes of the fusing of Greek and Hebrew, gospel and culture, Spurgeon and Horton. Barson of Penge was a noted liberal, but he claimed Spurgeon as a formative influence, with P.T. Forsyth as another. Forsyth, author of *Religion in Recent Art* (1887) and *Christ on Parnassus* (1911) had opened Penge with a sermon in 1912 and had married Herbert Ibberson and Kate Hewitt in 1893.[91] Frank Salisbury, who

---

[88] [A.D. Banfield], *Penge Congregational Church 1908-1958 - Golden Jubilee Celebration May 3-11th 1958*, pp.10, 13

[89] For Francis [Frank] Owen Salisbury (1874-1962) see Gray, *op.cit.*, p.316

[90] J.M. Young, 'Some Notes on the History and Building of Penge Congregational Church', ts. unpaginated, n.d. The setting of the originals is described and illustrated in F.O. Salisbury, *Sarum Chase*, rev.ed., 1953 pp.124-30, and B.A. Barber, *The Art of Frank O. Salisbury*, Leigh-on-Sea, 1936, pp.80-4

[91] For Peter Taylor Forsyth (1848-1921) see W.L. Bradley, *P.T. Forsyth, the Man and His Work*, 1952. He was the Hewitts's minister at Clarendon Park, Leicester 1888-94. Kate Mary Hewitt had joined the Church 21 February 1886 and was married there (Forsyth officiating) 8 September 1893

was from a Wesleyan family, joined Lyndhurst Road in July 1914.[92]

Such connexions, however contingent, allow us not just to chart the permeation of taste but to explain it. A Chapel of Youth would have been unthinkable in any Congregational church in 1892, when Ibberson began to practice. It was easily thinkable in 1932, when Ibberson's formulation of the concept might strike us as surprisingly old-fashioned. Perhaps this was as much in deference to its surroundings as to its memorial nature. This consistent good manners may be seen in his best domestic commission — a house for the Misses Melland — and in an institutional commission whose best expression never got beyond a letter to a nephew.

Mary and Annie Melland were the unmarried daughters of a Manchester-made cotton-bleacher turned banker. They were Congregationalists and denominationally well-connected. H.H. Asquith's first wife, the Helen Melland of his Maresfield Gardens and Lyndhurst Road days, was their first cousin and his sister continued to visit them. It may be that Hampstead lies behind Ibberson's commission to build in the Peak District; more likely it was a holiday in Hunstanton one hot Edwardian summer with Sunday service at Union Church.[93]

The Misses Mellands' father had retired from Withington, whose Congregational church he largely founded, to the Derbyshire rock whence most Mellands were hewn, Middleton-by-Youlgreave. There he leased the Regency gothick Middleton Hall and there he died, supposedly from germs lurking in its sanitary system. His daughters remained in the district. They were formidable women, well-read, musical, radical, socially advanced. Manchester mill-owner's daughter though she was, Mary Melland 'had always supposed that 'cotton mills stood in quiet open places outside the city'.[94] Her discovery that this was not so led to her work for the girls' club

---

[92] The Salisburys were Wesleyans in Harpenden. Frank and Maude Salisbury left Harpenden for Hampstead in 1913 and joined Lyndhurst Road 30 July 1914 (Church Roll 1897, now in Dr Williams's Library). Later Salisbury was associated with (the Methodist) Leslie Weatherhead's (Congregational) City Temple. His sitters included at least one member of Lyndhurst Road, Mrs William Garnett

[93] I am indebted to Mr D. Barton, Mrs K. Hooper, Mr N. Melland, Mr J. Rowland and Mrs Eleanor Sykes for recollections of Raenstor Close and the Misses Mary (1851-1938) and Annie (1858-1930) Melland

[94] *Mary Browne, 1851-1933*, ed. A.L. Arnold, priv., Manchester, n.d. (c.1934), p.26

(the first of its kind in Britain) in Lever Street, Ancoats. Raenstor Close, built in 1909-11, was where she recharged her batteries.[95]

The house, Raven's Tor indeed, commands a two-to-three acre site where the road climbs from Alport into Youlgreave. The prospects are glorious and the Close embraces them. It fits in in every way. The stone was quarried locally and wheeled up by hand. The slates are Cumberland slate. It was not large — library, drawing-room, five bedrooms — but it was built to last. There was thick felt in the roof, and up-to-date heating and water systems. At first none of the pipes was in lead, for Miss Melland had a terror of lead poisoning and it was only when the water from the excellent local well corroded her pipes and she was assured that lead pipes would not harm the supply that she gave in. The craftsmanship was local — Orpheus carved at the gates in deference to the musical ladies within; signs of the zodiac in plaster on the drawing-room ceiling — but the design was the architect's. Ibberson enjoyed the zodiac. His own drawing-room, when he had a house in Devon, had the zodiac in plaster on its ceiling. Ibberson's was the woodwork, left in its natural state, though subsequently painted, the comfy wing chairs and the firearms on the wall in the entrance hall. Ibberson's too were the gardens; vegetable, fruit, rose, herbaceous, terraced with gravelled walks and a stone pergola leading to a temple. Raenstor was a fully accoutred house-in-the-country. Its stables were built first, with a lodge for the gardener, while the Misses Melland lived temporarily at another family property in the village. Annie, lame from childhood and with a wooden leg, had charge of the gardens, and with their establishment of cook, parlourmaid, housemaid, coachman and three gardeners, she and Mary were Derbyshire's equivalent of the Misses Colman of Carrow Abbey.[96] They gave the village playing fields and a hall. They worshipped at the rum little Norman-style Congregational chapel, whose minister had taught evening classes in Greek and whose organist mystified all with his choice of tunes. They were horrified by the alien red tiles of their village's first council houses and they

---

[95] At a neighbouring country house, Lomberdale Hall, belonging to the similarly active (and Wesleyan) Mrs Waterhouse, P.T. Forsyth recharged his batteries for the writing of *The Soul of Prayer* (1916)

[96] Ethel Mary Colman (1863-1948) and Helen Caroline Colman (1865-1947), the unmarried daughters of J.J. Colman, were deacons of Princes Street; Ethel Mary was Britain's first woman Lord Mayor.

feuded satisfyingly with the local ducal landowner, Rutland, whose gardener they enticed for life in 1916 and whose land they bought whenever they could. Even their builder had the encouraging name of Gladstone Nuttall, and they backed Liberal candidates at election time though their reading led them well past women's suffrage and into the realms of theosophy and socialism.[97]

Raenstor Close is a Derbyshire house, generically Yorkobethan but not Yorkshire, not Cotswold, not Norfolk or Cambridge or Hampstead. Ibberson carried that localising knack into his institutional buildings, particularly at his old school, Bishop's Stortford, where he designed between 1909 and 1914 new classrooms and two houses, Grimwade (1913) and Alliott (1914).[98] The classrooms had a touch of meeting-house dignity, a slight red brick formality. Grimwade and Alliott belied their sound, for they were homely buildings, pleasantly down-beat reflections of the school's emergence into the country-boarding school swim of house spirit and carefully fostered tradition. They were characterised by caring little mannerisms. Alliott's Lower Dormitory had gaps in its tiled sills, each with a sloping shaft to the outside, to allow for ventilation. These could be closed by sliding a heavy tile across them. Ibberson had already tried this out at Chorleywood; surely his concern was prompted by memories of stuffy Stortford nights in the late 1870s? Another utilitarianly decorative vernacular touch, to be seen already in Hunstanton and at Chorleywood and to be repeated later at Elmers End and Recorder Road, is the decorative use of flint — cubes of flint popped into the half-brick gaps left when the scaffolding was removed.[99] This was a Sussex trick but Henry Wilson's friend, E.S. Prior, liked to use it.[100] It can be seen in another Ibberson building of 1914, the 'specially nice' gymnasium

---

[97] In 1924 the West Derbyshire Labour Party approached 'Miss Melland of Youlgreave' to see if she would be their candidate (either for Parliament or the County Council) or at least give financial support. They received 'no encouragement whatever'. Was this Mary (b.1851) or her anthroposophist niece May (b.1883)? West Derbyshire Labour Party, Minute Book 1924-37; 15 October 1924. I am indebted to Mrs M. Wilshaw for this

[98] Morley and Monk-Jones, *op.cit.*, pp.47-50

[99] I am indebted to Mr W.E. Hall and Mr G. Greatham for drawing attention to these features at the school

[100] Notably at what is now Home Place, Kelling (1904) in Norfolk where his chief associate was the Sussex-born Randall Wells (1877-1942)

which he built for Homerton, the originally nonconformist (and largely Congregational) women's teacher training college in Cambridge.[101] Here too Ibberson was humanising older buildings.

It was intended that he should design more buildings for his old school. There was a pressing need for a hall, to double as a chapel or whatever else in school life needed to hold large numbers. The challenge intrigued him and in 1917 he wrote about it to one of his two Baptist minister nephews, Wyndham Bryan's son Frank:

> After the war I hope to be up against the problem of a school hall at B.S.C. which will be also a school chapel — It must be solemn enough for communion services, gay enough for a school chantey — ('with a yo heave ho and a cheer for little Polly ...'!)
> I'm thinking of putting my communion table (and Cross if I can get it) in a recess under the organ, and to cover it with a gay curtain when social life is to the fore. I shall get plenty of light in the building and decorate largely in white which is both cheerful and solemn.[102]

We may now feel glad that the challenge did not come Ibberson's way. For whatever reason — and health is given[103] — his plans were abandoned and the commission for what was now a Memorial Hall on a different site went to that young architect errant, Clough Williams-Ellis. Posterity has become rightly proud of his stylish (indeed colourful, and thus controversial) essay in English baroque.[104] Nonetheless Ibberson's account in his letter to Frank Bryan of the challenge that never came is part of a further revelation of his own distinctive, instinctive, nonconformity. Like his father, Frank Bryan had a concern for worship's setting as well as its nature. He was a kindred

---

[101] Thus N. Pevsner, *The Buildings of England: Cambridgeshire*, Harmondsworth, 1956, p.185

[102] H.G. Ibberson to F.C. Bryan, 13 August 1957

[103] I am indebted to Mr W.E. Hall for this information

[104] As indeed was Clough Williams Ellis himself, since he noted that his Memorial Hall became 'the first building in England by a living architect to be scheduled for preservation'. C. Williams Ellis, *Architect Errant*, 1971, caption to illustration facing p.181. Ellis (b.1883) was in the news because of his contemporary conversion of Stowe to public school needs. See Morley and Monk-Jones, *op.cit.*, p.67 for the Hall built 1921-2; the controversial lapis lazuli interior decoration went in 1968

soul. R.F. Horton had officiated at his wedding in the chapel of Mansfield College, Oxford, and in 1917 he had a fine pastoral career ahead of him which was to culminate in the presidency of the Baptist Union in 1960-1. But in 1917 he was minister of Hope Chapel on Cardiff's Cowbridge Road, and he wanted to rebuild it. Hence Ibberson's letter, 'Train to Town Aug 13th 1917',

Dear Frank,
    That a nonconformist minister is interested in architecture, always rejoices my heart, that one tries to think it out on scientific lines has for me the delight of novelty. I'm new to it myself ...
    Well, about the house for the faith.
    I feel that we must insist on the holding up of the Lord in the sermon as a very important thing, the modern man will more and more be accessible through his brain. This means you must see and hear well — largely rules out domes which are acoustically bad, and pillars which hide the fair face of the minister. Pillars and arches which merely cut off the gangways are all to the good. The difficult thing for me is what are one's people to *look* at besides the minister. On the whole I don't think we can run to a chancel, we do not want a *sacred* screened off place for the altar and its ministrants where our Lord can be 'made and eaten all day long' — and to shut up a lot of women in hats in a starved and skimped apse has no reasonableness in it — Neither do I care to seem to worship pipes.
    I, in my present mood would carry the roof for its full height and width right on — but put the pulpit on one side and the organ on the other (or both) and have a great cross on the end wall, or a fresco of the resurrection. For thoughts come through the eye though less so than through the ear. Of course you can have a window, but windows properly treated are not very easily read, and I prefer strong light from the sides on a picture or emblem. I do not care for the table dead on the end wall — it is not for us an altar of sacrifice. I like your idea of the marble pool of baptism at the end, but it should be dominated by the Cross which belongs to us all ...
    As you say we have, or ought to have, the family feeling but at the same time we ought to want the feeling of awe in the presence of supreme love — If possible we should get it in two buildings — The church should not encourage conversation or thoughts of the details of one's neighbours life, but the Hall should encourage both. The hall should be a great place in our life and all that the tea meeting stands for should be run for all its worth, and so

should the prayer meeting.[105] In getting all we can from the catholics we must not lose what belongs to us especially — as you say in getting to grasp the idea of *the* church we must not lose the idea that we are a church.[106]

Here, midway between it and Chorleywood, was Elmers End to the life.

In the event Hope was not rebuilt in Frank Bryan's time there, and when it was (in most striking simplicity) it was not by Herbert Ibberson.[107] Yet in this letter we have the summation of his work (the chapel-meeting house at Chorleywood, the school buildings, the houses) and of the work to come (at Elmers End and Penge and Norwich). We have also that union of the catholic and the local, of spirit, word and symbol, which many Free Churchmen increasingly sought, especially in the 1930s.

When Ibberson died an appreciation called him a Puritan mystic:

> I remember once sitting with him in one of our typical chapels of the 'Nonconformist Doric' period, squat and ugly. When I remarked that it was like an old barn, he turned on me. Said he 'An old barn may be one of the most beautiful buildings on this earth. I would not exchange some of them for any of the sham Gothic places, with their pretentious vulgarity.'[108]

Nine years later Frank Bryan addressed the Baptist Union. His theme was 'The Sacraments':

> There are times when words fail, and feelings can best be expressed in deeds ... To seal a word spoken or a decision made, and to say things beyond the power of speech, to convey grace, to be a means whereby God communicates to us His very self.[109]

His were unusual words for Baptists, for though when 'practised in the form of immersion, baptism is a preaching of the Cross, the death, burial and

---

[105] This is the plan of Frank Lloyd Wright's Unity Temple, Oak Park, Chicago (1906)

[106] H.G. Ibberson to F.C. Bryan 13 August 1917

[107] By Ivor Jones and John Bishop of Cardiff, *BHB*, 1938, p.361

[108] J.C.H. 'A Master Builder', cutting dated 29 June 1935

[109] F.C. Bryan, 'Concerning Christ and His Church (c) The Sacraments', *Things Most Surely Believed*, 1944, p.71

resurrection of the Lord', not all would say that 'the core and climax of each sacrament is the ritual act.'[110] For Bryan communion was similarly limitless. 'We are one in the Communion of Saints. And the realisation of this in the Communion service is the Christian satisfaction of the heart.'[111] Then he came to earth, musing in the context of the Baptist May Meetings as he recalled

> 'my own father (a country minister) and some of his friends; I recall the grocer, the baker, and the linen-draper, men whose boots squeaked when they served at the Communion, who looked important when they took the collection, and rambled all over the place in their prayers, but who were pillars of the church, who loved the church ... They are gone from us now. But they are not dead.'[112]

Nine years before those words the architect, who might fitly have been added to that country minister's friends, had also gone. On the sun dial fixed to the entrance wall of The Gables, Ibberson's home in Austin Street, Hunstanton, were the words 'It is better to travel hopefully than to arrive'. He had now arrived.

V

There is a postscript, which might begin another architectural excursion. In 1904 Herbert Ibberson took into his London office a twenty-year-old just down from Caius, Cambridge, the younger son of his Norwich Baptist cousin John William Jewson, the timber merchant. This young man was Norman Jewson.[113]

Norman Jewson was with his cousin for three years and while there he learned about a family connexion of Kate Ibberson's, Ernest Gimson, who

---

[110] *Ibid*, pp.73, 74

[111] *Ibid.*, p.76

[112] *Ibid.*, p.78

[113] For Norman Jewson (1883-1975) see *The Times*, 10 September 1975

had been with Herbert in Sedding's office in the 1880s.[114] Jewson found Ibberson 'a charming man and a talented architect', but when he came across photographs of the cottages which Gimson had designed for his prosperous Leicestershire kinsfolk he knew that Gimson was superior 'to all other living architects whose work I knew'.[115] Norman did not follow his family's Baptist ways. His church observance, commissions apart, was restricted to rites of passage;[116] his conversion lay in discovering Gimson and when they met 'I felt that it had been the most wonderful and delightful day of my life'.[117]

It was August 1907. Jewson's apprenticeship was over, London was unbearable and he was on holiday, in a train which stopped at Cirencester. He got out. He had his sketch book, enough clothes, some books, a small tent, so he hired a donkey and trap. To go where? He let the donkey choose. So he came to Upper Slaughter. He stayed at The Swan, Chipping Campden. He walked in the North Cotswolds. And then he called on Ernest Gimson at Daneway House, Sapperton. 'Up to this time life as a young man training to be an architect had followed fairly normal lines' but

> the professional side of architecture had never appealed to me ... it was architecture I was interested in, not making a large income as an architect. My own buildings I wanted to have the basic qualities of the best old houses of their locality, built in the local traditional way in the local materials, but not copying the details which properly belonged to the period in which they were built.[118]

He stayed at Sapperton for the rest of his life, one of the Gimson, Barnsley, de Waals circle of Arts and Craftsmen, furniture makers, architects. He carved for May Morris at Kelmscott. He restored churches and houses. He learned to bake bread in a brick oven. And in 1911 he married Mary

---

[114] I am indebted to Mrs K. Hooper for confirmation that Kate Ibberson's cousin, Elisabeth Russell, married Josiah Mentor Gimson (1851-1925), Ernest Gimson's half-brother

[115] N. Jewson, *By Chance I Did Rove*, priv., 1973, pp. 1,15. One of the houses that so impressed him was for Mentor Gimson, Mary Comino, *op.cit.*, p.138

[116] I am indebted for this information to Miss Nancy Jewson

[117] Jewson, *op.cit.*, p.15

[118] *Ibid.*, p.13

Barnsley with his chapel kith and kin down from Norwich for his Cotswold Church wedding, the rector hurrying 'through the service at great speed, and it seemed to me that Mary and I were made man and wife in record time'.[119]

Although this exploration began with an ecclesiastical commission, and the growth of professionalism, especially among nonconformists, and although it ends with a young Cambridge man defying professionalism and his inherited Dissent alike for the liberating world of what is itself now almost a cult, a man of means working with his own hands and not going to church, I would suggest that the discontinuities are more apparent than real. The concern for a people's tradition is no discontinuity. While as for Mary Barnsley, her family background was as Wesleyan as her husband's was Baptist. His lay in Norwich timber; hers was in Birmingham building. John Barnsley and Sons built Birmingham's Council Houses; for the Wesleyans they built Handsworth College while at Tettenhall they built a West Midland version of Bishop's Stortford.[120] As for the Gimsons, though they were secularists from Leicester, there was a near branch of the family which was Baptist and in timber like the Jewsons. They too had their links in architecture, though theirs is not a Norfolk story, even tangentially.[121]

---

[119] *Ibid.*, p.93. Mary's father, Ernest Barnsley (1863-1926) and her uncle Sydney Barnsley 1865-1926), had been in Sedding's office

[120] See Mary Comino, *op.cit.*, pp.15-17. The doyen of the family's Methodism was General Sir John Barnsley (1858-1926), head of the family building firm and first cousin of Ernest and Sydney Barnsley. See *Who Was Who 1916-1928*, p.57. I am indebted to Mr R. Rose for alerting me to Sir John

[121] It is, in fact, a Sheffield story. Ernest Gimson, of the secularist branch, went to Franklin's school, Stoneygate, Leicester, whose founders and principals were Baptists

THE BROWNISTS IN BURY ST EDMUNDS

JOHN CRAIG

The 'Stirs' was the name given by contemporaries to the series of religious controversies centred on the town of Bury St Edmunds from the latter half of the 1570s to 1584. These controversies involved a variety of persons ranging from the Bishop of Norwich, Edmund Freke, and the Eastern Assize Judges, down to the neighbouring gentry, clergy, townsmen and local villagers and they have been interpreted in a number of ways. Most historians have focused on the fascinating wrangle between the Bishop and a group of godly Suffolk magistrates led by Sir Robert Jermyn and Sir John Higham. Overlooked in this emphasis is the part played by the Bury townsmen and specifically by a group of Brownists.

Historians of Dissent need no introduction to Robert Browne, the details of whose life have generated much discussion and plenty of spilt ink. Best known for his work of 1582, *A treatise of reformation without tarying for anie*, Browne was one of the first to set out the principles of a gathered church, independent of both Crown and Parliament. Between the formation of a Congregational church in Norwich in 1579 and its departure to Middelburg by 1582, Browne preached throughout East Anglia and in 1581 was active in Bury, a town already deeply divided over religious issues.

Two puritan ministers, John Handson and James Gayton, proved the object of much dissension in the town. An entry into the 'godly' community in Bury is provided by three surviving petitions sent by almost two hundred townsmen between 1578 and 1582, either to Lord Burghley or to the Privy Council, pleading for the reinstatement and continuance of the two preachers. Surviving wills and subsidy rolls were examined to identify as many of the petitioners as possible. Identification of about sixty-five of the petitioners has made it possible to examine the question of whether the 'puritanism' of the Bury petitioners was 'Brownism'.

The question is an important one. At the Summer Assize of 1583, the

Crown executed two Brownists, John Copping and Elias Thacker, both of Bury, and publicly burnt books written by Browne. Earlier, a group in Bury had compared Queen Elizabeth to Jezebel by painting the warning of the angel to the church of Thyatira (Rev. 2:19) around the Queen's arms in the parish church of St Mary. Moreover, Archbishop Whitgift later described the 'Stirs' in Brownist terms, as a time 'when the pretended Reformation was begun there, without staying for the magistrate, as the term was then'. Some of the petitioners clearly were Brownists as the surviving evidence makes plain.

Viewed more broadly, however, there is little evidence that the 'puritanism' of most petitioners was fuelled by Brownist sympathies. The bequests made by most of them mirrored those of the godly magistrates, finding common ground in their support for godly preachers and for the parish library founded in Bury in 1595.

The story of the Bury Brownists ended in failure. But if Brownism is merely seen as an ecclesiastical blip that reverted to a form of conservative Calvinism expressed in institutional forms, this may overlook the extent to which Brownist sympathies had radicalized borough politics. For while the efforts of the Bury petitioners on behalf of their preachers served in the short term at least to solidify the place of godly magistracy in Bury, those same efforts carried an implicit challenge to the place and authority of the gentry magistrates that found its expression in the townsmens' drive for incorporation and expressed confidence in their abilities to govern themselves. Perhaps at this point, the 'puritanism' of the Bury townsmen owed much to the influence of the Brownists.[1]

---

[1] A full version of the above paper is published under the title of 'The Bury Stirs Revisited: An Analysis of the Townsmen', *Proceedings of the Suffolk Institute of Archaeology and History*, vol.xxxvii (3), 1991, pp.208-24

THE RELATIONSHIP OF EARLY MARKET TOWNS AND NONCONFORMIST CENTRES TO NINETEENTH CENTURY INDUSTRIAL DEVELOPMENT IN SUFFOLK

GWEN DYKE

Almost twenty years ago Professor Alan Everitt of Leicester University produced a paper entitled *The Pattern of Rural Dissent in the Nineteenth Century* which dealt principally with the counties of Kent, Leicestershire, Lincolnshire and Northamptonshire. He opened with the evocative statement

> The English have a genius for retaining the form of their institutions and traditions while transferring their substance. For a people not much given to hard thinking, this habit of mind creates a comfortable illusion of continuity, and a welcome sense of safety, in a dangerous world.

He went on to identify a loss of force and power represented by such insubstantial words as 'nonconformity' and 'Dissent'. Titles such as The Hallelujah Band, The Peculiar People, The Recreative Religionists, The Christians who object to being Otherwise Designated and the Wesleyan Reform Glory Band, in contrast, expressed 'restless consciences and urgent quests for more perfect societies' lacking elsewhere in the 1970s.

Important conditions cited by Everitt for the development of nonconformity were the presence of large amounts of extra-parochial or common land, the existence of decayed market towns, large parishes and the lack of a dominant squirearchy. When he proceeded to argue a correlation of rural Dissent with freehold property in direct succession to Domesday freeman holdings, and with the prevalence of small industries, it became a theory I wanted to examine in Suffolk.

I did this in a highly superficial way. Circumstances prevented further research, although I exchanged comments and information with Dr Everitt. So this paper must be seen as a provisional statement which may influence other historians to examine the theory and perhaps prove or disprove it by more scholarly research into East Anglia.

I took twenty-five Suffolk towns and villages with early market grants and tabulated the number of Domesday freemen, evidence of early nonconformity, nineteenth-century industrial developments and the number and character of Dissenting chapels. In so doing I left out nine coastal townships as atypical because of geographical changes; forty-five villages the trading ambitions of whose medieval landlords outran their powers of performance; and twenty-one places whose mercantile aims failed immediately.

The evidence is inconclusive, but there emerges a balanced picture of the successful Suffolk township - near the coast but not on it, possessed of an early, perhaps continuing market with associated fairs and with a notable percentage of Domesday freemen and burgesses. It had an early nonconformist history and by the nineteenth century, many Dissenting groups and their religious buildings. It also had a thriving nineteenth-century industrial record. Most have survived to this day as flourishing modern communities.

Some tentative conclusions may be drawn. Early markets based on freehold tradition thrived: Ipswich, Sudbury and Woodbridge display exceptional evidence in support of Everitt's theories. Towns under feudal or ecclesiastical masters were relatively static in medieval times, but forged ahead with marked independence once this dominant medieval power was gone: Bury St Edmunds, Bungay, Stowmarket, Framlingham and Leiston all demonstrated this clearly.

One fifth of the towns had recorded nonconformist traditions from the fifteenth-century Lollards onwards; three-fifths were noted centres of puritanism soon after the Reformation. These early origins are exemplified by the number and variety of later chapels and meetings. In Suffolk the comparative strength of the Society of Friends, and the bewildering variations on Baptist and Independent doctrine outweighed the ubiquitous Methodism of the Midlands; and while the exoticism of Catholic Apostolics, Swedenborgians and Episcopal Missionaries flourished in Ipswich and Hadleigh many other groups were to be found in the county's small towns.

The seventeenth-century decline in the wool and cloth trade was coupled with an early lack of freedom in such clothing towns as Hadleigh, Lavenham and Long Melford, and they did not bounce back as vigorously as, for example, Bungay, Woodbridge or even Wickham Market. The last is my

EARLY MARKET TOWNS AND NONCONFORMIST CENTRES

native village and the only one I have studied at any great depth. The manor never predominated in Wickham and ecclesiastical/political allegiances were never allowed to interfere with trade. Puritanism in the seventeenth century led to later resilience from industrial decline and the threat of domination by outside landlords, which I feel to be a sign of true nonconformity. In the nineteenth century numerous craftsmen moved in and adapted to the local engineering works, milling or ancillary crafts. The brickworks increased production, houses were built or rebuilt to house new workers. Retail trades and crafts, even schools increased to serve the new population.

But - the Dissenting interest was static. The settlement had only one Congregational chapel, a little mild Methodism, and later some activity from the Salvation Army and the Plymouth Brethren. The two last are the only survivors. I conjecture that the motive powers of Dissent and nonconformity were transferred to the trading activities as they adapted after the closure of the brickfield and the iron works. Service to East Suffolk farmers and gentry was the new way to prosperity. The duties of Good Service, High Ideals, Hard Work and Superlative Quality replaced more conventional religious themes. (It may be noted that the parish church has been as Low as possible for three centuries).

Who is to say which is more godly? To hold integrity through changes of aim and objective not only displayed their beliefs, but showed also their plain common sense, and ensured their survival in a changing world. At least thirty trade/craft families are still serving the community after a century of change, still with an ability to move against the tide. It would be interesting to know how other East Anglian townships compare. The Nonconformist Conscience is alive and well, though formal religious Dissent no longer plays any part in it; the power of resistance to worldly ideals and temptations is only disguised, not outgrown.

All over Suffolk chapels have gone though some yet keep their rigid adherents, slightly anachronistic but a power for good. The same power remains in the little old firms in little old towns, still making a respectable living, still doing a good job for very moderate rewards. They may be transmuted, but they are still active for good - and for God? - in their communities, and of shining integrity. As Selden said in 1689:

EARLY MARKET TOWNS AND NONCONFORMIST CENTRES

STATUS	PLACE	DATE OF MARKET	NO. OF FAIRS	% DOMESDAY FREEMEN	EARLIEST NONCON-FORMITY	NO. OF C19 CHAPELS	DENOMINA-TIONS	NO. OF C19 INDUSTRIES	1950 STATUS
EARLY BOROUGHS	East Beccles	pre 1066	2	50%	C15	6	I/C B WM PM RC SA	7	Market Town
	Eye	1086	2	54% *C	C15	2	B WM	4	Small Town County
	Ipswich	pre 1066	7	98%	C15	13	C P U B SPB WM PM RC M CAP SW SA Q	19	Market Town
	West Bury St Edmunds	pre 1066	5	54% *A	C15	11	B SPB C PM WM P U PB SA RC Q	7	Cathedral Market Town
	Clare	pre 1066	2	34% *C U	C15	3	I/C B (Q)	6	Lrg Village
	Sudbury	pre 1066	3	94% W	C17	6	B C PM RC SA (Q)	6	Market Town
EARLY MEDIEVAL TOWNS	East Bungay	1228	3	33% *C	C15	8	C B P/I PM RC PM WM SA	9	Market? Twn
	Debenham	1221	1	33%	C17	3	I/C SA M	4	Lrg Village
	Framlingham	1286	2	19% *C	C16	8	C U WM I PM UM CS RC	3	Market Town
	Halesworth	1222	3	33%	C18	4	I/C B PM M	7	Small Town
	Mendlesham	1238	1	33%	C16	3	B C (Q)	3	Lrg Village
	Needham Mkt	1226	1	16% LS	C16	4	C PB WM (Q)	4	Small Town
	Saxmundham	1272	1	17% *M	C16?	5	I/C B WM SPB SA	-	Market Town
	Stowmarket	1066	2	20% LS	C17	5	I/C B PM SBP RC	-	Market Town
	Stradbroke	1225	1	33%	C17	1		2	Lrg Village
	Woodbridge	1227	3	89%	C16	6	C B M SA RC (Q)	8	Market Town
	West Hadleigh	1245	3	12.5% W	C16	6	CUR B PM EPM SA RC	7	Small Town
	Haverhill	1086	2	33%	C16	6	I/C PM P B SA Q	6	Small Town
	Lakenheath	1201	1	33%	C17	4	I/C PM WM B C	1	Lrg Village
	Lavenham	1257	3	5% W	C17	4	I/C WM PM SA	3	Small Town
	Long Melford	1235	2	2% W	C16	2	C PM	4	Lrg Village
LATER MEDIEVAL TOWNS	East Leiston	1312	1	52% *A	C17	4	Q WM UM I/C (ME) (SA) (C) PB	2	Small Town
	Wickham Mkt	1370	3	89% LS	C16	4		8	Lrg Village
	West Mildenhall	1412	1	13%	C17	5	ME B WM CA (Q)	2	Small Town
	Woolpit	1381	1	66% *A	C17	2	PB PM	2	Lrg Village

146

EARLY MARKET TOWNS AND NONCONFORMIST CENTRES

KEY

NONCONFORMIST CHURCHES

I	Independent
I/C	Independent Congregational
C	Congregational
CUR	Congregational United Reform
CA	Calvinist
CS	Christian Science
CAP	Catholic Apostolic
B	Baptist
SPB	Strict/Particular Baptist
P	Presbyterian
P/I	Presbyterian Independent
PM	Primitive Methodist
WM	Wesleyan Methodist
UM	United Methodist
M	Mission (unspecified)
U	Unitarian
PB	Plymouth Brethren
SW	Swedenborgian
RC	Roman Catholic
Q	Quaker
Ep.M	Episcopal Mission
ME	Methodist Evangelical
SA	Salvation Army
( )	Indicates former denomination no longer active

* = Dominated by A abbey, C castle, M manor, W wool trade
LS = late settlement

Information for the nineteenth century from 1888 Directory of Suffolk

> The Puritans who will allow no freewill at all, but God does all, yet will allow the subject his liberty to do or not to do ... The Armenians, who hold that we have freewill, yet say there must be all obedience, and no liberty to be stood for. [1]

Perhaps the debt to our nonconformist tradition in East Anglia, and the latent power it has given us, is best known in the history of our small independent towns, their free citizens, their tradition of Dissent and their varied industries. J.R. Green got it about right:

> The mill by the stream, the tolls in the market place, the brasses of its burghers in the church, the names of its streets, the lingering memory of its gilds, the mace of its mayor, tell us more of the past of England than the spires of Sarum or the martyrdom of Canterbury.[2]

Many individual articles, guidebooks and municipal publications have contributed details to the table and evidence to the conclusions drawn, too many to list individually. The main sources are listed below:

Alan Everitt, *The Pattern of Rural Dissent: the Nineteenth Century*, Leicester, 1972
The Victoria County History of Suffolk, vol. II, Domesday Book.
N. Scarfe, *The Suffolk Landscape*, 1972, esp. ch.4
N. Scarfe, 'Suffolk Towns', *The Suffolk Review*, vol. 5, no.3, 1982
White's Directories, Kelly's Directories, esp. 1844, 1855, 1864, 1878, 1888, 1912, 1937.

---

[1] J. Selden, *Table Talk*, 1689, p.20 quoted in *Seventeenth Century England, A Changing Culture*, ed. Anna Hughes, vol.I, 1980

[2] J.R. Green, *A Short History of the English People*, 1895, p.xi

RECORDS OF NONCONFORMITY IN CAMBRIDGESHIRE

MICHAEL FARRAR

The National Surveys

Bishop's Returns, 1669 for Ely diocese (existing also for 1665 and 1676 elsewhere). Information for each parish of conventicles, the sect that used them, the number of people attending, their quality, and the names of teachers. Published in *Original Records of Early Nonconformity under Persecution and Indulgence*, 3 vols., by Professor G. Lyon Turner, 1911-14; analysed by parish, denomination and county.

Licences under Declaration of Indulgence, 1672 (in State Papers Domestic, Public Record Office). Three volumes of entry books and two albums of original documents (letters and memoranda). Published in *Original Records* (as above).

Survey of Presbyterian Congregations, 1690, arranged by counties. Published in *Freedom after Ejection* by Alexander Gordon, Manchester University Press, 1917.

List of Dissenting Meeting Houses and Roman Catholic Chapels by Dr John Evans, 1715-17, updated to 1730; at Dr Williams' Library (index published in *Dr Williams' Library Occasional Papers No.11*, 1964).

Revd Josiah Thompson's List of Dissenting Congregations by Counties, 1715 and 1773, at Dr Williams' Library (partly published in *Transactions of Congregational Historical Society*, vol.5, 1911-12, and *Transactions of Baptist Historical Society*, vol.ii, 1910-11).

Registration of Meeting Houses, either with Quarter Sessions or Bishop (or Archdeacon etc.) under Toleration Act 1689, originally mainly with Quarter Sessions, but later mainly with Bishop. Over a thousand new conventicles were built in twenty years after 1689. Among diocesan records at Cambridge University Library are petitions dated 1697-1700, 1717-20, 1722-30, 1736-

1850. At Record Office, Huntingdon, for 1691-1704 (eight) and 1780-1851 (337).

Return of Dissenting Meeting Houses in England and Wales, including Catholic, 1836, printed in Parliamentary Papers HC433 (1836) xl 267.

Ecclesiastical Returns, 1851 (H.O. 129 in Public Record Office). Returns of churches and chapels, endowments, sittings, estimated attendances on 31 March 1851 and average numbers during the preceding twelve months.

Types of Local Records

Church Book, typical of Baptists, Congregationalists and Presbyterians, although no uniformity. Often contains description of founding of the congregation and of invitation to minister(s), covenant and signatures of those binding themselves to it, minutes of church governing body, and quite often lists of members at intervals as the covenant is renewed.

Registers of nonconformists were mostly surrendered to the Registrar General in 1837 and are now in Public Record Office. Many of them no earlier than the nineteenth century. Linton Independent Chapel, built 1698, has registers from 1787 only. Very few are older than 1740.

Records of Particular Denominations in Cambridgeshire

Baptists

Records of Strict Baptist churches at Great Gransden (formerly Independent), including church book 1690-1775, described by H.G. Tibbutt in *Records of Huntingdonshire*, vol.i, 1969, (Huntingdonshire Local History Society), and of Kimbolton (also formerly Independent), including church books 1692-1962 and registers 1742-1817, have been deposited at the Record Office in Huntingdon. Records of Bottisham Lode (1809-1919) and Eden, Cambridge (1845-1979) have been deposited at the Record Office in Cambridge.
    Records of General Baptist churches deposited at Cambridge include those of St Andrew's Street, Cambridge (church book 1720-1856), Melbourn

(church book 1688-1784), Soham (minutes from 1770 and church book from 1840), and Cottenham (birth register 1789-1903, as well as the Cambridge and District Christian Education Council (formerly Sunday School Union) 1819-1979, while deposited at Huntingdon are records of Great Gidding 1781-1943 (including diaries of the pastor, Joseph Norris of Swavesey 1850, 1852-4), as well as of Huntingdon and District Sunday School Union 1930-70. Remaining at the churches are records from 1693 at Isleham, 1710 at Gamlingay and from 1742 at Haddenham, and, in Huntingdonshire, from 1690 at Great Gransden (formerly Independent) and 1786 at Bluntisham. Some Baptists records are in other repositories. Those for Whittlesey 1870-1966 are in the Lincolnshire Record Office, for Godmanchester from 1801 and for Kirtling from 1893 in the Gospel Standard Baptist Library at Hove, and for Benwick 1858, Cambridge Tenison Road 1897, Elsworth 1887, Hail Weston 1757, Stapleford 1851, Willingham First Chapel 1726, Cottenham Ebenezer 1793 and Somersham (date unknown) with the Strict Baptist Historical Society at Dunstable.

Congregationalists

Records deposited at the Record Office at Cambridge include those for Melbourn (church book from 1745 and accounts from 1789), Linton (church book from 1703 and register from 1787) and Great Eversden and Kingston (copy church book from 1775), while at Huntingdon there is Hail Weston (church book 1692-1710). Churches retaining records are known to include Emmanuel, Cambridge from 1720, Fenstanton and Warboys from 1644 (published in 1854 by the Hanserd Knollys Society), St Ives from 1742, and St Neots from 1724. Records deposited, however, include those of the Cambridge and District Free Church Federal Council 1912-87, of the Huntingdon Association of Baptist and Congregational Churches 1893-1966, and, in Cambridge, of the Railway Mission 1886-1972 and of New Street Bible Class 1902-88.

Religious Society of Friends (Quakers)

The national meeting was the London Yearly Meeting, while there were Quarterly Meetings in each county in the seventeenth century. In the years following 1750 these were often amalgamated. Deposited at the Record Office in Cambridge are records of Cambridgeshire Quarterly Meeting 1670-

1756 and Huntingdonshire Quarterly Meeting 1673-1756, and of the later Cambridgeshire and Huntingdonshire Quarterly Meeting 1756-1850. Monthly Meetings covered smaller areas, and records are at the Cambridge office for Cambridge (later Sutton) Monthly Meeting 1663-1782, for Isle Monthly Meeting 1656-71, Huntingdon Monthly Meeting 1672-1850, Wisbech Monthly Meeting 1758-85, Wisbech and Sutton (later Chatteris) Monthly Meeting 1785-1850, Cambridge and Huntingdon Monthly Meeting 1850-80, Cambridge, Huntingdon and Lynn Monthly Meeting 1880-1970, and Cambridge and Peterborough Monthly Meeting 1970-87.

The Quakers are notable among religious denominations for having always made and preserved meticulous records of their doings. One type of record that is unique to them is the record of sufferings - the punishments, fines and oppression that were inflicted upon them for refusing to support the established church or for publicising their beliefs.

Methodists

Deposited at the Record Office in Cambridge are records of the (later Wesleyan) Ely Circuit from 1796, of the Fenland Circuit from 1830, Cambridge Circuit from 1815 (when it was formed from Bury St Edmunds), Cottenham Circuit from 1877 (when it was formed from Cambridge) until 1884, Mildenhall (later Newmarket and Mildenhall, then Newmarket, Soham and Mildenhall Circuit) from 1828, and Thetford Circuit (Mildenhall Division) 1833-46, while at Huntingdon are deposited the records of Huntingdon (later Huntingdon and St Ives) Circuit from 1823.

Of Primitive Methodist records there are at the Cambridge office those of the Cambridge Circuit from 1823, Cambridge Second Circuit 1882-1910, Soham (later Soham and Ely, then Ely) Circuit from 1826, Soham Circuit from 1849, Wickhambrook (later Wickhambrook and Newmarket, then Newmarket) Circuit from 1857, Upwell and Manea Circuit from 1882, and Wisbech Circuit from 1926, while at Huntingdon there are the records of St Ives Circuit from 1860. The only United Methodist records represented are those of Christchurch Chapel in Elm from 1911. The records of Peterborough and Raunds Circuits are at the Northamptonshire Record Office.

Typical Methodist records are minutes of Quarter Day, becoming minutes of the Local Preachers' Meeting, and accounts, later becoming the Circuit Steward's Book.

THE DOCUMENTARY PROBLEMS ENCOUNTERED IN RESEARCHING THE HISTORY OF AYLSHAM BAPTIST CHURCH

A.G. ALLCOCK

When I was asked to write the history of the Baptist church in Aylsham as a basis for a publication marking the two hundredth anniversary of its foundation, I thought that I had a relatively easy assignment. Being a Baptist church and, therefore, responsible for its own records, I felt that all the information I would require could be obtained from the Minutes of Deacons and the Minutes of Church Meetings. The two meetings should record all the problems and decisions taken throughout the years.

My first disappointment came when I discovered that there were no Minutes of Deacons' Meetings available. A minute book was in being for so-called Church Meetings, but this did not start until 1823 and even then someone had 'written it up' more in the form of a journal. It was not until well into the nineteenth century that it makes a precise record of decisions taken.

Fortunately, one of the early Deacons had made a copy of the deeds and a record of the transfer of the meeting-house and adjoining cottage in 1826 from the ownership of the minister to the chapel trustees for the sum of £225. The original deed was deposited with the Baptist Union of Great Britain, but this copy has been kept by the family of one of the Deacons who had signed the deed. There was also a copy of Proudfoot's broadsheet which was found in a schoolroom. This described the formation of the church by Dr Joseph Kinghorn, the minister of St Mary Baptist church, Norwich.

My first task was to seek information from the records of that church. These are kept in the Norfolk Record Office, but, unfortunately, there was little here that was relevant to my researches. However, in a minute book there is a reference to people leaving St Mary's and joining a meeting in Aylsham as early as 1787.

I was fortunate enough to mention my difficulties to Mr Molland, the custodian of Norwich Cathedral Library. He directed my attention to the letters of Dr Joseph Kinghorn in the biography by M.H. Wilkin.[1] Amongst these letters are those between Joseph Kinghorn whilst he was minister at St Mary's and his father, also a minister. He described his part in the baptism of five people by total immersion in the River Bure at Aylsham at 4 am on 22 April 1791.

Two cottages were converted into a meeting place for the Baptist group. Increasingly Dr Kinghorn came to use the building not just for Sunday services, but also to give instruction on Christian doctrine and Bible study and a regular fellowship was formed. There is a copy of the original document which turned the building into a formal Baptist chapel. Kinghorn also details in his letters the subsequent turbulent hostility towards Dissenters in Aylsham culminating in the appearance of Joseph Kinghorn before the Norwich magistrates to give evidence against the rioters. The magistrates confirmed him in his possession of the land and building.

Surviving minute books note details of the extension of the chapel in 1833 prior to the construction of the baptistry; schoolrooms were added in 1876. The chapel was renovated in 1983 and further rooms added in 1985. The Manse was bought from the Methodists in 1883.

The membership roll records the names of the five people baptised in the River Bure in 1791. By 1835 membership had grown to ninety-two and by 1888 there were 102 members on the roll. In the same year 174 children and twenty-six teachers were listed in the Sunday School.

Further details of the history of Aylsham Baptist church can be found in the booklet produced to mark the chapel's bicentenary[2] whilst useful secondary sources are Sapwell's *History of Aylsham*,[3] and histories of the Baptists in Norfolk.[4]

---

[1] M.H. Wilkin, *Joseph Kinghorn of Norwich*, Norwich, 1855

[2] A.G. Allcock, Joyce Chapman and Tony Bartlett, *Aylsham Baptist Church: Bicentenary 1791-1991*, Aylsham, 1991

[3] A. Sapwell, *History of Aylsham*, Norwich, 1960

[4] C.B. Jewson, *The Baptists in Norfolk*, 1957, and M.F. Hewett, The History of Norfolk Baptists, a collection of material in preparation for a historical record of the Baptists of Norfolk and their church, 3 vols, mss notebooks, NRO 1942/7

A NONCONFORMIST DESCENT

JOHN LE GRICE

It is perhaps significant that nonconformity, once firmly established within a family, often survived and flourished from generation to generation. Its outward form might vary between individuals and the particular denominational allegiance of family members might change, yet a Dissenting attitude of mind remained.

Alice Sarah Wood of Cambridge, my grandmother, who married Charles Clements Le Grice of King's Lynn, inherited a copy of the *Memoirs of John Meadows*,[1] a minister ejected from the Rectory of Ousden, Suffolk, in 1662. The *Memoirs* were compiled by Edgar Taylor (1793-1839), a descendant of John Taylor (1694-1761) minister to the congregation who built the Octagon Chapel in Norwich. Richard Taylor married Margaret, a granddaughter of John Meadows.

My research has linked the Meadows of the *Memoirs* with the Wood family of Cambridge and hence with the Le Grice family. A major source of information has been the collection of Non-Parochial Registers in the Public Record Office. The Meadows were associated with Rushmere, Witnesham and Chattisham in the fifteenth century. Daniel, who married Elizabeth Smith of Wickham Market, died in 1651 and is buried in Chattisham church. Three of their sons graduated from Emmanuel College, Cambridge. Philip (1625-1718) undertook diplomatic business and was knighted by Charles II. His descendant was created Earl Manvers in 1806. John (1622-96) was the subject of the *Memoirs*.

John remained in Cambridge as a Fellow of Christ's College until 1653 when he resigned, became Rector of Ousden and married Anne Rant of Swaffham Prior. He was ordained in 1657 by the Presbyterian method. When the 1662 Act of Uniformity required episcopal ordination of all clergy,

---

[1] Edgar Taylor, *The Suffolk Bartholomeans: A Memoir of the Ministerial and Domestic History of John Meadows ...*, 1840

A NONCONFORMIST DESCENT

John refused and was ejected from the living at Ousden. Initially he was allowed to live at Ousden Hall where he provided accommodation for other ejected ministers, but later he settled in Stowmarket. Here his wife died in 1675 and he later married Sarah Fairfax who was the mother of his seven children. Sarah was the niece of a Cambridge friend who had been ejected from Barking cum Needham and was a descendant of John Fairfax, who had been made Master of the Great Hospital, Norwich in 1609. Sarah died in 1688. John spent the last years of his life at Bury assisting the Presbyterian minister there. His third wife was Anna Beaumont of the Bildeston family.

The eldest son of John and Sarah was another John (1676-1757) who became minister of the Presbyterian church at Needham and remained there for fifty-six years. He and his wife, Sarah Chaplin (1675-1732), are buried in Barking church. Hannah, his daughter, married Thomas Fuller of Audley End and Mary, his youngest (1714-1802), married Samuel Wood.

Daniel and Philip, younger brothers of John of Needham, became Freemen of Norwich. Philip was Mayor in 1734 and his daughters married into the Taylor and Martineau families.

There were three Presbyterian ministers in Suffolk named Samuel Wood. Samuel I (1683-1748) was pastor at Wivenhoe in 1707 and later at Lavenham, Bishop's Stortford and Woodbridge. Extracts from his diary were published in the *Congregational Magazine* in 1834. Samuel II (1710-67) was minister at Sweffling and later at the Old Meeting House, Norwich where he and his wife are buried. Samuel III was minister at Framlingham from 1740 to 1756. He married Mary Meadows in 1744.

Samuels I and III were father and son; Samuel II was a 'kinsman'. All were present at Framlingham in 1744 when Samuel III was ordained. Also present was Dr Philip Doddridge who trained ministers at Northampton. Doddridge's published letters include correspondence with the Woods.

Seven children are recorded as born to Samuel and Mary Wood at Framlingham. The youngest, Thomas, born 1754, was living at Dallinghoo when his son Thomas was born in 1787. This latter Thomas opened a music and piano shop in Market Street, Cambridge around 1825.

I have been unable to identify the mother of his two children Mary Elizabeth (born 1825) and Thomas Meadows (born 1827), but Thomas married again in 1837 to Catherine Bradford Nutter. The Nutter family were Baptists and in later years Thomas Meadows Wood and his family, including my grandmother, attended the Chesterton Baptist church. Thomas Wood is mentioned in the biography of Sterndale Bennett, the pianist and composer, as a 'friend, well known music seller and organiser of local concerts'. Thomas Meadows Wood became a pupil of Bennett's and taught music in Cambridge. Later he took over the music business, by then situated in St Mary's Passage.

Thomas Meadows Wood married Sara Clear in 1856. They lived at first in Trumpington Street and later in Warkworth Street, Cambridge. My grandmother (1866-1953) was the youngest of five children.

A QUAKER IN LOCAL POLITICS: WILLIAM GRAVESON 1862-1939

VIOLET ROWE

Since his mother was a Salter and his paternal grandmother a Hoyland, both well-known Quaker families, it is not surprising that William Graveson attended a Quaker school - Ackworth - and was apprenticed to a Quaker firm - Shewells of Darlington. At twenty-one he came back home to Hertford to run the family drapery business there. At once he brought new life to the moribund Liberal party in the town where the Tory Marquess of Salisbury was politically powerful, and the Liberals had not even nominated a candidate to the Borough Council for six years. Graveson won his first political victory in 1884: all the four vacant seats were won by Liberals assisted, no doubt, by the effect of the Corrupt Practices Act of the previous year.

Graveson did not stand for election himself, however, for another twelve years - shops were open for seventy to ninety hours a week at that time and this left little opportunity for politics. He worked hard for the Society of Friends and for the Adult School movement, but these were weekend activities. It was not until 1901, and after one unsuccessful attempt, that Graveson gained a seat on the Borough Council. He had been nominated by men from both parties and by ten women (though he was not a supporter of women's suffrage at that time). For the next eighteen years he was active in civic affairs and by 1913 he was also a County Councillor.

In 1919, however, he faced an unexpected challenge for his County Council seat from Noel Pemberton Billing, a Midlands aeroplane manufacturer who had wrested the East Hertfordshire Parliamentary seat from the Tory grasp and who now aimed at capturing a County Council seat as well. Graveson defended himself and his pacifist beliefs with vigour and his usual sense of humour. He acknowledged Billing's outstanding abilities, but he more than matched his rival's flair for publicity and pro-Graveson posters, with an effective caricature of Billing, flooded the town. The Quaker won by nearly fifty votes though Billing's noisy supporters drowned his rival's victory speech, and for twenty years Graveson retained his County Council seat. He died in 1939, alderman and vice-chairman of the County Council and among the many tributes that his widow received was one from Charles Holden, the distinguished architect of London University Senate House buildings; another came from the retired housekeeper of the days when the family and staff lived above the shop. It was to 'Mr William, my best friend in the world'.

INDEX

Ackworth School	158	Barnsley, General Sir John	139, 140, 140fn
Adelaide Place, London	116	Barnsley, Sidney	104, 140fn
Adriaenssen, Cornelius	33	Barson, Ernest	129, 131
Alby, Norfolk	78	Bartas, - du	34
Algoet, Antonius	22	Barton Turf, Norfolk	38
Allen, J.	82	Bawdeswell, Norfolk	87, 88
Allen, Thomas	38	Beaumont, Anna	156
Alport, Derbyshire	133	Bebbington, D.W.	90, 91
Amersham Hall School	109, 109fn	Beccles, Suffolk	106, 108, 146
	110, 113	Beckenham, Kent	116, 126, 128fn, 129
Ampthill, Bedfordshire	121	Beckenham Congregational Church	
Amsterdam	12, 30, 34, 36		128fn, 129
Ancoats, Lancashire	133	Beckley, James	122
Antwerp	29	Beer, Devon	126fn
ArchaeologicalJournal	14	Belcher, John	114-6
Arch, Joseph	78, 79, 85	Belgravia, London	101
Architectural Association	100	Bellamy, Edward	118
Ashwicken, Norfolk	37	Benacre, Suffolk	77
Asquith, H.H.	117, 132	Bennett, Sterndale	156, 157
Audley End, Essex	156	Benwick, Cambridgeshire	151
Aylsham, Norfolk	70, 78, 153, 154	Bermondsey, London	129
		Bexhill, Sussex	96
Baker, Herbert	110	Bible Christians	48fn
Balkius, Isbrandus	22	Bildeston, Family	156
Baptists	11, 12, 19, 20, 38, 39, 42	Billing, Noel Pemberton	158, 159
	43, 44, 48, 51, 52, 60, 63, 70, 96, 98fn,	Binfield, Clyde	67
	101, 102, 107, 108, 113, 114, 119, 120,	Birmingham	140
	123, 124, 125, 126, 128, 135, 137, 138,	Bishop's Stortford, Hertfordshire	156
	139, 140, 140fn, 144, 147, 149, 150,	Bishop's Stortford College	103, 105
	151, 153, 156	109, 113, 134, 135, 140	
Baptist May Meetings	138	Blakeney, Norfolk	51
Baptist Union of Great Britain	136, 137	Bloomsbury, London	107, 110
	153	Bluntisham, Huntingdonshire	121, 151
Bardsey, Samuel	41	Boardman Family	113
Barford, Norfolk	41	Boardman, Arthur	103
Barker, Joseph	80	Boardman, Bruce	103
Barking, Essex	156	Boardman, Clement	103, 104
Barking-cum-Needham, Suffolk	156	Boardman, Edward	102, 103, 104, 106-9
Barnard, Mr	16	111, 112,	
Barnes, Frederick	20	Boardman, Edward Theobald	102, 103, 104
Barningham, Suffolk	108	106, 109, 110, 111, 112, 113	
Barnsley, Ernest	104, 140fn	Boardman, Ernest Charles	103, 104, 106

Index

Boardman, Florence *née* Colman	110, 104, 112	Bylaugh, Norfolk	79
Boardman, Howard Whittier	103		
Boardman, Humphrey Colman	104, 112	Cadogan Estates, London	110
Boardman, James	103, 104	Calvin, John	31
Boardman, John Alexander	103, 106	Calvinism	52, 129, 142, 147
Boardman, Wilberforce	103, 106	Calvinistic Methodism	43, 44
Bonnell, Family	26	Cambridge	113, 116, 121, 134, 149-52, 155, 156, 157
Bottisham Lode, Cambridgeshire	150		
Bourne, Henry	74	Cambridge:	
Bowman, Thomas	43, 44	Gonville and Caius College	131, 138
Bradfield, Norfolk	38	Christ's College	155
Brandon, Suffolk	111	Emmanuel Church	151
Brandon Parva, Norfolk	40	Emmanuel College	155
Breccles, Norfolk	38	New Street Bible Class	151
Briggs, Martin	67	Railway Mission	151
Brighton, Sussex	116	St Andrew's Street Baptist Church	150
Bristol	114, 115	Society of Friends	151-2
Briston, Norfolk	42	Tenison Road Baptist Church	151
Brock, William	107	Cambridge and District Christian Education Council	151
Brooke, Thomas	32		
Brown, Charles	125	Cambridge and District Free Church Federal Council	151
Brown, Florence	125		
Browne, John	38, 42, 43	Canterbury, Kent	27
Browne, Robert	141	Cardiff: Hope Chapel	136, 137
Brownists	141-2	Carrow Abbey, Norwich	112, 133
Brundall, Norfolk	41	Carter, Mr	98
Bryan, Caroline *née* Jewson	104 121	Catholic Apostolic Church	144, 147
Bryan, Revd A. Keith	104	Cawston, Norfolk	44
Bryan, Frank	104, 135-8	Centre of East Anglian Studies University of East Anglia	59
Bryan, Wyndham Colin	104, 120-1, 122-3, 135		
		Chamberlain, A.J.N.	87
Builders' Journal	123	Chaplin, Sarah	156
Bungay, Suffolk	106, 108, 144, 146	Charles II	155
Bure, River	154	Chatteris, Cambridgeshire	152
Burghley, Lord	141	Chattisham, Suffolk	155
Burial Acts 1847, 1857, 1880	69	Chenies, Buckinghamshire	109
Burnham Market, Norfolk	41	Chesterton, Cambridgeshire	156
Burnham Overy, Norfolk	41	Chicago, USA	137fn
Burston, Norfolk	41	Chipping Campden, Gloucestershire	139
Bury St Edmunds, Suffolk	9, 14, 15, 20, 111, 141-2, 142fn, 144, 146, 152, 156	Chorleywood Hertfordshire	122-5, 129, 134, 137
Bury St Edmunds: Churchgate Street Chapel	14, 15, 16	Chorleywood Baptist meeting house	125
Butterfield, William	100	Christians Who Object to Being Otherwise Designated	143

161

Index

Church of Christian Science	93, 94, 96, 147	Cruso, Jan	34, 36
Church of England	74	*Daily Telegraph*	118
Church of Latter Day Saints	48fn, 51	Dallinghoo, Suffolk	156
Cirencester, Gloucestershire	139	Dathenus, Petrus	31
Clapton, London	117	Davie, Donald	91
Clare, Suffolk	146	Davy, Widow	38
Clarke, Ann	38	Dawber, E. Guy	110
Clarke, H.W.	73, 74	Debenham, Suffolk	146
Clarke, Joseph	14	de Carle Family	103, 105
Clear, Sarah	157	de Carle Smith, Joseph	105
Clemence, John Louth	106, 107, 110	de Carle Smith, Priscilla *née* Boardman	103, 104, 105
Cley, Norfolk	43		
Clowes, William	74	Defoe, Daniel	14, 16
Cobbett, William	77	del Corro, Antonio	31-2
Colchester, Essex	115	De la Forest, -	32
Colens, Lydia	25	Denton, William	41
Colens, Michiel	25, 25fn	Desbonnet Family	26
Colkirk, Norfolk	41	Dickleburgh, Norfolk	38
Collinges, John	13	Diss, Norfolk	37, 38, 40, 51
Collins, William	101	Dobson, Barbary	40
Colman, Ethel Mary	133, 133fn	Dr Williams' Library	149
Colman Family	109	Doddridge, Dr Philip	75, 156
Colman, Helen Caroline	104, 133, 133fn	Docking, Norfolk	41
Colman J.J.	103, 104, 110-1, 112, 120, 133fn	Dolby, G.W.	63
		Domesday Book	143, 144
Colman, Russell	111, 112	Downham Market, Norfolk	41, 42
Colman, Laura	104, 112	Dublin	116
Congregationalists	12, 17, 51, 60, 63, 73, 75, 96, 100, 101, 102, 105, 108, 109, 111, 113, 114, 116, 117, 119, 126, 128, 129, 132, 133, 135, 141, 145, 147, 150, 151	Dunstable, Kent	151
		Dunthorne, John	38
		Dutch	21-8, 29-36
		Ealing, London	116, 123
CongregationalMagazine	156	Earith, Huntingdonshire	121
Conventicle Act, 1593	12	Eastbourne, Sussex	82, 91
Copping, John	142	Eastbourne: Pevensey Road Chapel	73
Corpusty, Norfolk	38	East Dereham, Norfolk	40, 41, 42, 79, 86-8, 96fn, 109
Corrupt Practices Act, 1883	158		
Corton, Suffolk	111	East Dereham: Cowper Memorial Church	108-9, 109fn
Cottenham, Cambridgeshire	151, 152		
Countess of Huntingdon's Connexion	43-4, 48fn, 52, 100, 101, 103	East Harling, Norfolk	43
		Eastern Assize Judges	141
Cozens-Hardy Family	109	*Eastern Weekly Leader*	89
Cromer, Norfolk	88	*Eastern Weekly Press*	82, 85
Cromwell, Oliver	16, 81, 117	Eden, Cambridgeshire	150

162

Index

Eddy, Mary Baker	94, 95, 96, 98fn	Friston, Suffolk	19
Edmondson, James	101	Fuller, Thomas	156
Edwards, George	78, 79-81, 83, 84, 85, 88-9, 91		
		Galliart, William	30
Elison, John	29, 35, 36	Gamlingay, Cambridgeshire	151
Elizabeth I	21, 32-3, 142	Garnett, Mrs William	132fn
Elm, Cambridgeshire	152	Gayton, James	141
Elmers End, Kent	126-9, 130, 134, 137	George, Ernest	109-10, 115
Elsing, Norfolk	79, 90	George, Henry	118
Elsworth, Cambridgeshire	151	Gibson, Dan	110
Ely, Cambridgeshire	103, 152	Gibson, Henry	86
Ely Diocese	149	Gimson Family	140
Emden	30	Gimson, Ernest	115, 120, 138, 139, 139fn, 140fn
Episcopal Missionaries	144		
Everett, Zachariah	80	Gimson, Josiah Mentor	139fn
Everitt, Alan	143, 144	Gissing, Norfolk	43
Eye, Suffolk	111, 146	Glemsford, Suffolk	11
		Glemsford:	
Fairfax, John	156	Ebenezer Chapel	11
Fairfax, Sarah	156	Providence Chapel	11
Fairfax, Sir Thomas	35	Glover, the Misses	41
Fakenham, Norfolk	40, 41, 78	Godmanchester, Huntingdonshire	151
Feaver, Alfred	129	Godwin, E.W.	114
Fenland Wesleyan Methodist Circuit	152	Golders Green, London	116
Fenstanton, Huntingdonshire	151	Grantham, Thomas	38
Ferme Park, London	101, 125	Graveson, William	158-9
Fersfield, Norfolk	43	Great Ellingham, Norfolk	41, 42, 43
Figgis, John Benjamin	116, 116fn	Great Eversden, Cambridgeshire	151
Figgis, John Neville	116, 117fn	Great Gidding, Huntingdonshire	151
Figgis, Mrs Phillips	116-7	Great Gransden, Huntingdonshire	150, 151
Figgis, S.	117	Great Ryburgh, Norfolk	41
Figgis, Thomas Phillips	116, 117fn, 129	Great Yarmouth, Norfolk	12, 13, 20, 29, 37, 38, 40, 41, 42, 43, 48, 64, 106
Filby, Norfolk	37, 38		
Finsbury Park, London	101	Green, J.R.	148
Fisher, Mary	38	Greenwich Palace	32
Flanders	31	Grindal, Edmund, Bishop of Norwich	32
Fleetwood, Lieutenant General	16	Grover, John	101, 122
Flemings	21-8, 29, 33, 36	Guestwick, Norfolk	14-5, 16, 38, 51
Forncett St Peter, Norfolk	41	Gurney Bank	108
Forsyth, Peter Taylor	131, 131fn, 133fn	Gurteen Family	105, 111
Framlingham, Suffolk	15, 144, 146, 156	Gurteen, Catherine *née* Boardman	103, 105
Free Church	116, 126-8	Gurteen, Daniel III	105
Free Methodist	111	Gurteen, Daniel IV	105
Freke, Edmund, Bishop of Norwich	141	Gurteen, Daniel V	105
Fressingfield, Suffolk	19		

Index

Haddenham, Cambridgeshire	151	Hunstanton: St Edmund's Chapel	119
Haddiscoe, Norfolk	41	Union Church	119-22, 132
Hadleigh, Suffolk	144, 146	Hunt, John	40
Hail Weston, Huntingdonshire	151	Huntingdon	150, 152
Halesworth, Suffolk	108, 111, 146	Huntingdon, Countess Selina	43, 44
Hallelujah Band	143	Huntingdon Association of Baptist	
Halstead Times	105	and Congregational Churches	151
Hampstead, London	116, 117, 131, 132, 134	Huntingdon Society of Friends	152
Hampstead Hill Gardens, London	118	Huntingdon and District Sunday	
Handsworth College	140	School Union	151
Harleston, Norfolk	37, 38, 108	Hunworth, Norfolk	41
Harpenden, Hertfordshire	132fn		
Harrison, Samuel	78, 80	Ibberson Family	113, 119, 121
Harrow School	110	Ibberson, Charles I	104, 121
Haverhill, Suffolk	105, 106, 111, 146	Ibberson, Charles II	104, 121
Haywards Heath, Sussex	82	Ibberson, Harriet *née* Jewson	104, 121
Heacham, Norfolk	41	Ibberson, Herbert George	96, 97-8, 98fn
Hertford	158	102, 113-6, 117-21, 123, 125-31, 126fn,	
Hewitt Family	119, 119fn	32, 133, 134, 135, 136-7, 138-9	
Hewitt, Arthur Leicester	120fn	Ibberson, Kate Mary *née* Hewitt	
Hewitt, Francis	119	104, 119, 121, 131, 138, 139fn	
Henricipetri, Adam	34	Ibberson, Mary *née* Jewson	104,
Higham, Sir John	141	Independents	12, 13, 14, 16, 19
Handson, John	141	38, 39, 42, 43, 48, 51, 63, 105, 106, 128	
Highbury, London	101	144, 147, 151	
Highbury College	114	Independent Labour Party	91
Hindhead, Surrey	101, 122	Indulgence, Declaration of 1672	13, 47
Hingham, Norfolk	51	51, 149	
Historical Atlas of Suffolk	47	Ingham, Norfolk	42
Holden, Charles	159	Institute of British Architects	99
Holme Hale, Norfolk	43	Ipswich, Suffolk	14, 16, 103, 144, 146
Holt, Norfolk	40, 41	Ipswich:	
Homerton College, Cambridge	135	Green Yard Chapel	16
Honing, Norfolk	38, 41	Portman Road Presbyterian Chapel	20
Hook, John	43	St Nicholas Street meeting house	
Hopkinson Family	114		14, 15-6, 19
Horder, Percy Morley	129	Stoke Green Chapel	19
Horder, Thomas	119, 129fn	Tacket Street Chapel	16, 20
Horton, Robert Forman	117-8, 122, 131, 136	Irmingland Hall, Norfolk	16, 40
Hove, Sussex	151	Isle, Cambridgeshire	152
How Hill, Norfolk	112	Isleham, Cambridgeshire	151
₊Hoyland Family	158	Islington, London	117
Hughes, Hugh Price	90	Ivory, Thomas	18, 102
Hunstanton, Norfolk	116, 119-22, 123, 125		
126fn, 131, 132, 134, 138			

Index

Jamieson Family	118
Jarrold Family	106
Jermyn, Sir Robert	141
Jessop, Revd Augustus	84
Jewson Family	106, 113, 118, 121, 140
Jewson, Revd Arthur	104
Jewson, C.B.	38, 43
Jewson, Ethel *née* Boardman	103, 106
Jewson, George I	104
Jewson, George II	104
Jewson, Harriet Jessie *née* Hewitt	96, 96fn 97
Jewson, Herbert	96, 96fn, 121
Jewson, John William	104, 138
Jewson, John Wilson	104
Jewson, Mary *née* Barnsley	139-40, 140fn
Jewson, Norman	102, 104, 138-40, 139fn
Jewson, Percy	104, 106
Jobson, F.J.	67, 68
Jolly, Cyril	43
Kelling, Norfolk	134fn
Kelmscott, Oxfordshire	139
Kenninghall, Norfolk	37, 38
Kensington, London	101
Kensington Palace Gardens, London	107
Key, Robert	80
Kilham, Alexander	79
Killingworth, Daniel	38
Killingworth, Grantham	38
Kimbolton, Huntingdonshire	150
King's Lynn, Norfolk	29, 37, 38, 40, 41, 42, 43, 48, 51, 113, 121, 155
King's Lynn Society of Friends	152
Kinghorn, Dr Joseph	153, 154
Kingston, Cambridgeshire	151
Kirkpatrick, Thomas	13
Kirtling, Cambridgeshire	151
Knott, A.G.	126fn, 127
Labour Party	90, 91
Ladbroke Grove, London	116
Lakenheath, Suffolk	146
Lasco, Johannes à	21, 27
Lavenham, Suffolk	144, 146, 156
Laxfield, Suffolk	11
Le Grice Family	155
Le Grice, Charles Clements	155
Leicester	119, 140, 140fn
Leicester: Clarendon Park Congregational Church	96fn, 119
Franklin's School Stoneygate	140fn
Leicester Mercury	119, 119fn
Leiston, Suffolk	144, 146
Lenwade, Norfolk	58
Lewes, Sussex	82
Lewis, Reginald	131
Leyden	12
Liberal Party	158
Lingfield, Surrey	116
Lingwood, Norfolk	43
Linton, Cambridgeshire	150, 151
Little Walsingham, Norfolk	19
Loddon, Norfolk	40, 41, 43
Lollards	9, 144
London	14, 23, 30, 31, 32, 110, 116, 139
London Congregational Union	126
London: Dutch Church	21, 23, 31
University	159
Long Melford, Suffolk	144
Looking Backward	118
Lowestoft, Suffolk	77, 106, 107, 108, 110
Lowestoft - St Mary's Church	142
Lucas, Charles	107-8, 110, 113
Lucas, Peto	107
Lucas, Thomas	107-8, 110, 113
Ludham, Norfolk	112
Lutyens, Edwin	20, 110
Lyndhurst Road Congregational Church	117, 119, 126, 132
Lyng, Norfolk	88
Maidenhead, Berkshire	118
Manchester	114, 132
Manea, Cambridgeshire	152
Manvers, Earl	155
Maresfield Gardens, London	118
Marshall, Ellen	104

Index

Marsham, Norfolk	78	National Agricultural Labourers' Union	78
Martham, Norfolk	43, 44	79, 85	
Martin, Basil	118	Needham, Norfolk	43
Martin, Kingsley	118fn	Needham, Suffolk	146, 156
Martineau Family	156	Netherlands	27, 29, 30, 34
Mattishall, Norfolk	38, 83, 86	New Church	48fn
Meadows, Daniel	155	Newcastle, Northumberland	35, 36
Meadows, Hannah	156	Newmarket, Suffolk	152
Meadows, John I	155, 156	*News from Nowhere*	118
Meadows, John II	156	Niebuhr, H. Richard	75, 76, 78, 81, 82
Meadows, Mary	156	89, 91	
Meadows, Philip I	155	Norfolk and Norwich Amalgamated	
Meadows, Philip II	156	Labourers' Union	78, 79
Melbourne, Cambridgeshire	150-1	Norfolk Archaeological Rescue Group	59
Melland, Annie	132-3	Norfolk County Council	79, 86
Melland, Helen	132	Norfolk, Duke of	33
Melland, Mary	132, 134fn	Norfolk Farmers' Labour Defence	
Melland, May	134fn	Association	87
Melton, Suffolk	20	Norfolk Federal Union	79, 85
Mendham, Thomas	41, 42	Norfolk and Suffolk Yacht Club	108
Mendlesham, Suffolk	146	Norris, Joseph	151
Methodists	9, 19, 20, 40, 42	North Lopham, Norfolk	40, 41, 86
43, 52, 58, 60, 63, 73, 74, 80, 84, 89		North Tuddenham Friendly Benefit	
90, 140fn, 144, 145, 152, 154		Society	79, 82, 83
Methodist Conference	79	North Walsham, Norfolk	37, 38, 43
Methodist New Connexion	74	Northampton	156
Miall, Edward	85	Northwold, Norfolk	43
Middleburg	141	Norton Subcourse, Norfolk	42
Middleton-by-Youlgreave, Derbyshire	132-3	Norwich:	9, 13, 21, 29, 30
Mildenhall, Suffolk	111, 146, 152	31, 32, 33, 34, 35, 36, 39, 40, 41, 43	
Mill Hill School	103, 106, 126fn	44, 48, 51, 52, 88, 91, 103, 105, 106	
Mills, C. Wright	75, 78	107, 108, 113, 121, 137, 140, 141, 156	
Mitchell, Arnold	110	Norwich:	
Molland, Mr	153	Ber Street Wesleyan Chapel	108
Moody, Dwight Lyman	84	Calvert Street Chapel	101
Moore, Abraham	38	Castle	80, 108
Moore, Robert	91	Cathedral Library	153
Morgan, Mr	97-8	Chapelfield	80
Morris, May	139	Cherry Lane Chapel	43
Morris, William	115, 118	Crown Point House	111
Morton, Revd H.C.	73-4, 91	Diocese of Norwich	37
Moser Family	118	Dutch Church	23, 29, 30, 33, 35, 36
Muswell Hill, Middlesex	101	East Granary, Blackfriars' Monastery	23
		Foundry Chapel	39
		French Church	26

Index

Goat Lane Meeting House	101-2
Great Hospital	156
Guildencroft Meeting House	13-4
Jenny Lind Hospital	108
London Street Improvement Society	108
Magdalen Road Congregational Church	111
Motor Company	96
Norfolk and Norwich Hospital	108
Octagon Chapel	13, 18, 93, 101 102, 155
Old Meeting House	13-4, 101, 106, 156
Presbyterian Congregation	13, 18
Princes Street Congregational Church	101, 102-5, 108, 111, 133fn
Recorder Road Christian Science Church	92, 93-8, 134
Rosary Cemetery	70
St Andrew's	29, 30, 32, 33
St Edmund's	13
St George's Tombland	13
St Giles'	37
St James'	37, 38, 40
St John de Sepulchre	40
St Mary Baptist Church	101, 102 105, 106, 153
St Paul's	37, 39
St Peter Mancroft	40
St Stephen's	13, 39
Tabernacle	43
Theatre Street Presbyterian Church	108
Unthank Road Baptist Church	108
Walloon Church	33
West Granary, Blackfriars' Monastery	13
Noyes, John	11-2
Nuttall, Gladstone	134
Nutter, Catherine Bradford	156
Osborn, Francis	41
Oulton, Norfolk	16, 37, 38
Ousden, Suffolk	155-6
Outlook	128fn
Overstrand, Norfolk	20, 112, 113
Owen, Robert	118
Oxford	116
Oxford: Mansfield College	136
Paton, J.B.	116
Paton, John Lewis	117fn
Patterson, Arthur	64
Peckover, Joseph	42
Peculiar People	143
Peterborough	152
Pettingale, Samuel	40
Pilmoor, Joseph	43
Pitt, William	69
Plymouth Brethren	48fn, 52, 145, 147
Presbyterians	13, 14, 15, 16 18, 20, 38, 51, 81, 108, 116, 147, 149 150, 155, 156
Primitive Methodists	19-20, 44 48fn, 52, 63, 64, 74, 76, 78, 79, 82, 84 86-91, 147, 152
Proudfoot, -	153
Pulham Market, Norfolk	37, 38, 39
Pulham St Mary Magdalen, Norfolk	37, 38 39, 43
Peckover's Bank	108
Penge, Kent	117, 129, 131, 137
Perowne, John	41, 43
Peto, Harold	101, 110
Peto, Sir Samuel Morton	107-9, 110
Peart, Mr	82
Pocock, W.F.	101
Pocock, W.W.	101
Poor Laws	77
Prior, E.S.	115, 134
Privy Council	141
Ramsey, Huntingdonshire	113
Rant, Anne	155
Raunds, Northamptonshire	152
Reading, Berkshire	109, 113, 114fn, 118
Reading: St Mary's Castle Street	113
Recreative Religionists	143
Redenhall, Norfolk	38
Reepham, Norfolk	86
Religious Census 1851	48-58, 150

Index

Rembrandt	29, 36
Rendham, Suffolk	17
Rickman, Thomas	100
Rickmansworth, Hertfordshire	121-2
Ridley Bax Family	118
Ritchie, James Ewing	77, 81
Rix, George	78-9, 81, 83, 85-8, 89-90
Rix Family	106
Roberts, Ann	38
Rockeghems, Remens van	25
Robins, Joseph	40
Roman Catholics	126, 128, 147, 149, 150
Royal Academy Schools	113, 116
Rupert, Prince	35-6
Rushmere, Suffolk	155
Russell, Elizabeth	139fn
Rutland, Duke of	134
Ryckwaert, Carolus	22
Sabbatarianism	82, 84
St Ives, Huntingdonshire	151, 152
St Martin's Lane, London	116
St Neot's, Huntingdonshire	151
Salisbury, Frank	131, 132fn
Salisbury, Marquis of	158
Salisbury, Maud	132fn
Salter Family	158
Salvation Army	145, 147
Sandemanians	48fn, 52
Sapperton, Gloucs	139
Sapwell, A.	154
Saxmundham, Suffolk	146
Saxthorpe, Norfolk	38
Sankey, Ira David	84
Scarning, Norfolk	84, 86
Schultz, R. Weir	110
Scott, Baillie	120
Scott, Sir Gilbert	100
Scott, Master	35
Scott, Mr	96
Sedding, John Dando	114-5, 116, 123, 139, 140fn
Selden, J.	145, 148
Sellars, Ian	60, 69, 72
Semmel, Bernard	74
Seth-Smith, Howard	101
Shadford, George	41, 43
Sharrington, Norfolk	41
Shaw, Norman	101, 115
Sheffield	140fn
Shelfanger, Norfolk	20
Shewells of Darlington	158
Shrewsbury School	117
Sloane Street, London	115, 123
Smallburgh, Norfolk	37, 38
Smith, Elizabeth	155
Smith, Thomas	20
Smith, Mr	83
Society of Friends	12, 13, 17, 41, 42, 43, 47, 48fn, 51, 63, 100, 102, 128, 144, 147, 151, 152, 158
Soham, Cambridgeshire	151, 152
Solemne, Anthony de	29-36
Somerleyton, Suffolk	107
Somerman, Jacob	24fn
Somersham, Huntingdonshire	151
Southampton, Hampshire	101
South Creake, Norfolk	41, 42
Southery, Norfolk	38
Sparham, Norfolk	80
Spelman, Edith née Boardman	103, 105
Spelman Family	106
Spelman, W.W.R.	106
Sprowston, Norfolk	91
Spurgeon, Charles Haddon	122, 131
Spurgeon's Pastors' College	121
Stamford Hill, Middlesex	101, 122
Stapleford, Cambridgeshire	151
Starkey, A.P.	96, 97
Stephens, Mr	82
Stowmarket, Suffolk	144, 146, 156
Stradbroke, Suffolk	146
Strangers	21-8, 29, 32, 33, 34
Stratford East, London	103
Street, A.E.	116
Strype, John	31
Stuart, James	112
Sudbury, Suffolk	144, 146
Sutton, Cambridgeshire	152
Sutton, Surrey	95, 96

Index

Swaffham, Norfolk	51
Swaffham Prior, Cambridgeshire	155
Swafield, Norfolk	17, 18
Swanton Abbot, Norfolk	38
Swanton Morley, Norfolk	79
Swedenborgians	52, 144, 147
Sweffling, Suffolk	156
Switzerland	31
Taylor Family	156
Taylor, Ann	38
Taylor, Edgar	155
Taylor, Dr John	18, 155
Taylor, Margaret	155
Taylor, Richard	155
Test and Corporation Acts 1829	69
Tettenhall, Staffordshire	140
Thacker, Elias	142
Thetford, Norfolk	29, 152
Thorpe-next-Haddiscoe, Norfolk	43
Thorpe-next-Norwich, Norfolk	38
Tibenham, Norfolk	38, 41
Titchwell, Norfolk	40, 41
Toleration, Little Act 1811	69
Toleration Act 1689	15, 37, 69, 149
Tory Party	158
Troup, Francis	120
Tunstead, Norfolk	38
Tubbs, Cyril Bazett	113-4
Tubbs, George Ibberson	113-4
Uniformity Act 1662	155
Unitarians	14, 48fn, 51, 63, 101, 102, 128
United Methodists	147, 152
United Reform Church	147
United States of America	152
Upper Slaughter, Glouctershire	139
Upwell, Norfolk and Cambridgeshire	52, 152
Vondel, -	35-6
Voysey, C.F.A.	120, 122, 123, 124, 125
Waals de -	139
Wacton, Norfolk	41

Walloons	21-8, 29, 31, 33
Wallwyn Family	26
Walpole, Suffolk	12, 15
Walsingham, Norfolk	41
Walters, Daniel	41
Warboys, Huntingdonshire	151
Ward, Mr	83
Warminster, Wilts	114
Waterhouse, Alfred	100
Waterhouse, Mrs	133fn
Watford, Hertfordshire	122
Wattisfield, Suffolk	15
Watts, Isaac	81
Watts, Michael	39
Waveney, River	48
Weatherhead, Revd Leslie	132fn
Webb, Aston	100
Webb, George	113, 114
Weeting, Norfolk	38
Wellingham, Norfolk	42
Wells-next-the-Sea, Norfolk	41
Wells, Randall	134fn
Wesley, Revd John	9, 18-9, 39, 41, 42, 43, 44, 58, 68, 74, 76, 90, 102
Wesley Guild	83
Wesleyan Methodists	48fn, 52, 58, 73, 87, 101, 103, 108, 132, 140, 147, 152
Wesleyan Reform Glory Band	143
Wesleyan Reformers (Branch)	48fn, 52, 58, 87
West, Alfred	109
West, Ebenezer	109
West Walton, Norfolk	37
Whalle, Thomas	22
Wheatley, James	39, 43
Whepstead, Suffolk	20
Whitfield, George	100
Whitgift, John, Archbishop	142
Whittlesey, Cambridgeshire	151
Wickhambrook, Suffolk	152
Wickham Market, Suffolk	144, 145, 146, 155
Wilkin, M.H.	154
Wilks, Mark	43-4
Williams-Ellis, Clough	135, 135fn

Index

Willingham, Cambridgeshire	151	Wood, Samuel II	156
Wills Family	114	Wood, Samuel III	156
Wilson, Bryan	75	Wood, Thomas I	156
Wilson, Henry	115-6, 123, 134	Wood, Thomas II	156
Wilton Family	106	Wood, Thomas Meadows	156-7
Winfarthing, Norfolk	37, 38, 41, 43	Woodbridge, Suffolk	17-8, 144, 146, 156
Wingfield, Suffolk	108	Woodford Green, Essex	103
Wisbech, Cambridgeshire	108	Woolpit, Suffolk	146
Wisbech Society of Friends	152	Woolwich Arsenal, London	108
Withington, Lancashire	132	Worstead, Norfolk	38
Witnesham, Suffolk	155	Wright, Frank Lloyd	137fn
Wivenhoe, Essex	156	Wright, Margaret	38
Wood Family	155-6	Wymondham, Norfolk	38, 40, 41, 42, 86
Wood, Alice Sarah	155		
Wood, Edgar	120	Yare River	34
Wood, Mary Elizabeth	156		
Wood, Mary	156	Zurich	27
Wood, Samuel I	156	Zwingli, Ulrich	27